Outlaw Aesthetics

OUTLAW AESTHETICS

Arts and the Public Mind
fred e. h. schroeder

Bowling Green University Popular Press
Bowling Green, Ohio 43403

Calib: Be not afeard; the isle is full of noises,
Sounds and sweet airs, that give delight and hurt not.

Copyright © 1977 Bowling Green University Popular Press

LC 77-71934

ISBN: 0-87972-085-9, clothbound
0-87972-086-7, paperback

Dedicated to those I love, the quick and the dead.

Contents

Contents

Foreword

Any book as eclectic as this must owe much to many; but any book as personal in style as this is should be cautious about acknowledging the ideas and criticisms of others, for such contributions become integral parts of the background of thought and expression, probably indiscernable even to those who contributed the original germ. Therefore, aside from the credits given in the chapter bibliographies, I will acknowledge help in only the most general terms. To my friends and colleagues in popular culture studies in the United States, Canada and the United Kingdom I extend thanks not only for the sympathetic ears they have given all these chapters when they were presented in oral forms, but for the ideas I have gleaned from their presentations as well. To my family, I extend thanks for the conversations and pleasant disputes that gave birth to many of the main concepts herein. All criticisms have been thoughtfully weighed; some have been accepted, some rejected, and many more have been altered to fit my purposes. Certainly any faults are mine, for I have been close to the manuscript all the way to final proofreading, and the editing and the design of the book are my own doing.

Two chapters have been published previously, one in the Western Humanities Review, the other in Fishwick and Browne's Icons of Culture. Both have been expanded in this book. Final manuscript typing was done by Marian Braff through the generous support of the College of Letters and Science of the Duluth campus of the University of Minnesota. Proofreaders were Cris Levenduski and Rex Levang, and preliminary typescripts were prepared by Ardys Grandstrand, Marie Knope and Cris Levenduski. I am especially grateful to Ray and Pat Browne for their encouragement in bringing this manuscript finally to press. This book was begun in 1970; it was fixed into type in 1976. But to complete it, I must refer you to the Afterword.

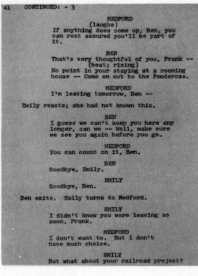

he fracas at the top is a wrestling "ballet" from the 1970s; the one below is from a W.C. Fields lm of forty years earlier. There is little difference in design, and in both, good and evil are efined clearly and simply for the audience. The shooting-script pages from two popular elevision series of the 1960s show the essential difference between a video aesthetic and an udio aesthestic. Each page is the thirty-eighth of its script, but the upper page is shot 41 (all onversation), while the other page contains seven camera shots in all, and the accumulated ots are three times greater than in the other script.

One, two, three!
Father ran.
Dick ran.
Jane ran.
They ran to Mother.

9

Entertaining and appealing publications for the children of well-to-do families were developed by John Newbery of London in the late eighteenth century, but as an aspect of American popular culture, with its own outlaw aesthetics, juvenile books and magazines had to await steam-presses, universal literacy and mass-marketing, all developments of the decades of the mid-nineteenth century. Despite many predecessors to the Scott, Foresman publishers' "Dick and Jane," the realistic continuing story about an average family of four or five did not catch on until around 1930. One aesthetic reason for the popularity of Dick and Jane is indicated above: their stories and pictures showed more action and a greater degree of humor than did their competitors'. In addition, the illustrations were brightly colored. Few educational publications drew directly on "outlaw" techniques. The Cordts Reader of 1929 is an exception, showning direct derivation from comic strip art.

THE FAMILY

Do you see the family?
Find Father and Mother.
Find Mother and Baby.
Bob and Betty love Father.
Bob and Betty love Mother.
Bob and Betty love Baby.
Do you love a baby?

Look, Mother! Mother, look!
See Baby walk!
Baby can walk.
Father, Father! Look, look!
See Baby walk to me!
Walk to Mother, Baby.
Oh, you funny little baby!

14   15

RIDING TO THE CITY

I

BOB: See those boys playing football!
BETTY: It must be fun to play football.
        How do you play it?
BOB: Oh, you run and kick.
        It is a fine game.
BETTY: I think it is more fun to ride
        to the city.
94

at time is it, Mother?
time to go home now.
e, children, we shall go.
you have a good time?
Mother, we had fun.
went to the big woods.
went with Grandfather.
had some apples to eat.
und eggs for Grandmother.
aw the kid.
is so little.
50

I like it here, Grandmother.
You have so many chickens.
You have so many eggs.
I like to find the eggs.
I like the big apple tree.
I like the apples on it.
We had a good time.
We like to come to see you.
We shall come again.
51

ספר התלמיד

20

בַּבֹּקֶר הַשֶּׁמֶשׁ יוֹצֵאת.
הַשֶּׁמֶשׁ נוֹתֶנֶת אוֹר.
הַשֶּׁמֶשׁ זוֹרַחַת.
יִצְחָק מִתְעוֹרֵר.

42

he Kendall Primer of 1917 was the first to employ realistic, contemporary content, along with a
ontinuing cast of characters.   This aesthetic style requires regular updating, and thus the
wentieth-century primer provides a plain and simple guide to changes in the predominant values
f the nation.   In 1917, children visit the city; in 1928 they visit the farm.   Even minority
ublications reinforced the majority values.   Like all other realistic primers, the 1926 Hebrew
eader emphasizes cleanliness, modern plumbing and homes located on open land-plots.

NEW! Natural-look "Instant Shrubbery"

MAKES THE FAST DIFFERENCE YOU WANT

This revolutionary landscaping is described on opposite page

The democratic yard is an open statement for all to see. Characteristically it is arranged for the pleasure of outsiders rather than for the owners. The mail-order catalog "instant shrubbery" follows this pattern, as does the plastic madonna in the bathtub grotto. In the display yard of a dealer in lawn ornaments, a plastic reproduction of a bathtub capitalizes on the outlaw creativity of the popular "junk aesthetic."

BOYS' OWN BIRD-HOUSES.

he wall built of tin-cans and the abstract sculpture of tire-casings (more correctly, a driveway marker and post-bumper) are in a tradition leading back to Harriet Beecher Stowe. The bir- houses for children are from her magazine, *Hearth and Home*, the planter made from a castoff x-muzzle is from an early domestic science book Mrs. Stowe and her sister. The contemporary oilet planter combines junk, lighthearted originality, and the medieval tradition of craft icons: his is attached to the sign for a plumber's shop.

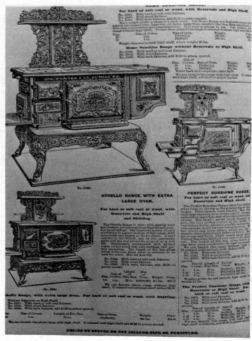

Icons are windows to transcendent realities. The nineteenth-century Mexican retablo, the con
temporary Indian chromo and the Sears Roebuck catalog page share the same aesthetic style.
Totally devoid of overall "artistic" design, each expresses a promise of a better life in simple
images that communicate ambiguous, complicated, profound truths to an unsophisticated
audience. *La Mano Poderosa* and *The Birth of Buddha* alike show the reduction to formula of
hands and faces. The three cooking ranges, in descending order, are *Home Sunshine*, *Perfect
Sunshine*, and *Othello*. The ornamentation not only indicates "artistic taste," but effectively
obscures imperfections in metal casting.

Protestant Christian religious art often emphasizes the act of worship rather than the object of worship. One of the most popular religious pictures today is *Grace*, by the early twentieth-century Minnesota photographer, Eric Enstrom. The composition probably derives from the Victorian British photograph, *Day's Work Done*, by Henry Peach Robinson. Albrecht Durer's drawing, commonly called *Praying Hands*, has undergone countless permutations, some of which border on kitsch. The illustration shows Durer reduced to salt-and-pepper shakers. The posing of Jesus in Holman Hunt's *Prince of Peace* has continued to the present day in best-selling versions by American artists. The anonymous sacred heart chromo (with hand-painted flames) probably dates from about 1925, but the almost feminine, blond visage doubtless derives from the nineteenth-centruy German academician, Heinrich Hofmann, best known for his painting of Christ in Gesthemane.

The "gift book" of art reproductions is one of the middlebrow popular arts. From Gustave Doré's *Bible Gallery* for the Victorian parlor table to Norman Rockwell for the cocktail table the pattern has persisted: expensive, large, realistic, anecdotal works that are unmistakeable in message, and usually unimpeachable in technical quality. The reproduction here is from a gift book associated with the World's Columbian Exposition. The limited edition is one answer to an American dilemma: how to have exclusive art that satisfies popular tastes. The figurines here are faultless in craftsmanship, but perpetuate popular sentimentality among the wealthy. Nevertheless, the high prices and limited availability, along with the social security of highbrow magazine advertisements obscure the family resemblances to souvenir dolls, run-of-the-mill Victorian academicians, and religious chromos. In the 1968 Sears Roebuck Christmas "wishbook" a $1600 suit of Toledo steel is paired with $2.62 shirts, high quality either way.

The Aesthetics of Popular Culture

While I was writing the chapter on popular garden ornaments for this book, I presented an informal slide-lecture on landscape art to the local Women's Club. At the close of the lecture, an elderly lady came to scold me, gently, for having "talked" sociology rather than art. There was validity to her criticism, as the pages following will bear out, but I will yet insist that this volume contains nearly all the major arts, and that they are my primary topics. Theatre, dance, painting, sculpture, literature and landscape architecture are all here as subjects of major importance, but sometimes they may be hard to recognize, for they appear in such forms as <u>Mission Impossible</u>, professional wrestling, Sacred Heart chromos, painted truck tires, and first grade readers. Arts they are, but they are arts of mass society. In that respect, then, this is a book of sociology.

To be somewhat more precise, this is a book about aesthetics - the philosophy of taste -; and about American studies - the investigation of our national character -; and about popular culture - the social, psychological and material environment of the majority of the people. At times, this book will be about a combination of all three subjects which might be called American popular aesthetics, but it would be

unfair so to label the whole book, because to do so would tend too much toward narrowing the scope of my intent.

Questions of aesthetics and the human response to the arts are found throughout the world and throughout history, but they have commonly been the province of a cultivated class of patrons and critics who are men and women of leisure, wealth and education. Four factors, however, have augmented the class of patrons, and these factors continue to increase that patronage at a rate of acceleration that appears to be destined to end in total uniformity or in infinite atomization, either of which might be an undesirable utopia. The accelerating factors are: democracy, the wider distribution of wealth, and mass industry and mass communication. The product of these factors is a well-to-do equalitarian populace that is served by mass industry and bound together by mass distribution and communication. Theirs is a new kind of culture, which can be called popular culture to distinguish it both from traditional local folk culture, and from sophisticated, privileged culture. This popular culture, along with its four contributing factors, is especially pronounced in the United States of America, and although it is now observable virtually worldwide, the popular culture phenomenon is equated with Americanization, even in those Western European countries which most resemble the United States.

Thus, a book about American studies can very much be of international and universal significance, and a book about popular culture can contain significant problems of the arts. To be sure, there are differences between the usual discussions of aesthetics and the discussion of popular culture aesthetics, but these are not differences of substitution or of omission. They are differences founded on the addition of three considerations to the discussion: these are market, manufacture and money. From these derive the essence of popular aesthetics: if the product sells, it is good art; if it does not, it is bad art. Whatever else I have to say is either expansion or qualification of that simple commercial standard of beauty: that which sells is beautiful in the popular eye, that which does not sell, is not beautiful.

Critics of the popular arts, that is, those who object to popular arts, are aware of this apparent criterion of taste, and they read into it a

2

commercial plot to lower the standards of taste in the people by giving them the cheapest, most tawdry, stereotyped and vulgar product possible. There is no such plot in operation anywhere in the world, though there are cheap, tawdry, stereotyped and vulgar popular products and arts. These, however, exist only where there is a market for them. If the audience will not buy, they will cease to exist.

This simple introduction should not be taken as an indication that an investigation into popular aesthetics is simple nor that the aesthetics of mass production are simple. Far from it. Indeed, it is possible that popular aesthetics is a more complicated subject than classical aesthetics, because there are more variables in the determination of what will sell well, and therefore be beautiful. One complication arises from the fact that we cannot play the game of searching for an absolute standard for beauty, nor even for an absolute standard for beauty in a given art form. The beauty of popular arts is always relative, relative to audience and relative to market. In practice, of course, all arts have some relativity to form and some higher criticism of the arts suggests to me that the ideal for aesthetics is creative art in a vacuum: an artist with total freedom, and with a will toward complete expression. Absolute freedom of expression does not exist and most of us, like Wallace Stevens, would rather judge the beauty of a work of art relative to contingencies, whether these are but the flaws of nature; or contingencies of the self-imposed type of the poet, who asks what liberty can be expressed in fourteen lines of iambic pentameter of three quatrains and a couplet; or of the outwardly imposed type of contingencies that confront the architect: what liberty can be expressed on the land-parcel provided with a budget of half-a-million dollars.

The contingencies of popular arts are nearly all like those of the architect, outwardly imposed by commercial requirements. What is the competion? What is the capacity of the retail outlets? What can be wrought without retooling? What limitations on quality are dictated by the manufacturing processes? What does the consumer expect? How far can the producer deviate from the consumers' expectations? What is the available capital? What is the maximum amount that consumers will pay? These are but a few of the restrictions that are imposed upon the artist-creator in the world of popular arts. Two instances of how these have operated in two different

3

popular arts may clarify the point. First, in automotive design, when Volkswagen expanded its line from the beetle to the bread-loaf, presumably a total redesign of body, it rescued the headlamps from the beetle and turned them sideways to fit the reversed curve of the bread-loaf body. In other words, economy in production costs affected the otherwise revolutionary change in design, and thereby restricted freedom of design. For a second example, consider the change in design of the Coca-Cola bottle from its classical shape in the $6\frac{1}{2}$ - ounce size to larger sizes. The increased size was dictated by the competition from producers of 12-ounce beverages - Royal Crown and Double-Cola, for instance. The continuation of the Coca-Cola bottle shape was dictated by the conservative expectations of the customers. But one unvarying contingency was the standard crown cap needed in the bottling plant to fit the machinery, and needed by the consumer to fit his bottle opener, and ultimately, probably dictated by the size of the human mouth. The aesthetic result was a sacrifice of proportion in bottle design. In the 16-ounce bottle, for example, the assertive and practical curve to the bottle, which fitted the human hand nearly perfectly, was reduced and elongated in sort of an El Greco effect; while in the quart bottle, the broad shoulder reduced the crown top to a pinhead, in sort of a Gaston Lachaise effect.

The examples I have given might be taken as touchstones for popular aesthetics, because both Volkswagen and Coca-Cola are internationally popular designs that have won the affection and later the approval of patrons of the established arts. Neither design was initiated to please aesthetically, for both were born of functional efficiency, and economical mass production techniques. Both were aimed at a mass market without any claim of exclusiveness, aristocracy or modishness. Both have a human dimension, the Coke bottle of hand and mouth, the Volkswagen of the whole body. They both gained popular acceptance without any bullying by tastemakers, and they both can be validated as art works according to the prevailing aesthetics of the twentieth-century, one way or another related to the Bauhaus.

The Volkswagen and the Coke bottle might be taken as touchstones for popular aesthetics, but it would be hazardous to do so. They are sculptural and utilitarian, and it would be difficult to transfer practical sculptural values to literature or music, not only because of the

4

three-dimensional concreteness of sculpture, but because the popular arts are for entertainment, recreation, and spiritual sustenance, not for containing liquids or passengers. So long as we limit our inquiry into popular aesthetics to utilitarian mass-produced objects, we may indulge in the higher aesthetics of form-follows-function, and we may judge all industrial design together, whether it comes out of Bauhaus, Dansk, Olivetti, or Coca-Cola.

Aside from the aesthetics of industrial design, which today is more often than not the conscious work of designers who are schooled in arts, my investigations seem to point to the almost total inapplicability of established aesthetic standards to the popular arts. Indeed, to apply classic standards is very nearly pointless, because when we hold the popular art work to the standard of the cultivated art work, it is invariably found to be wanting. It makes for an easy life, of course, the easy life that most of us were schooled in, wherein all products of culture are divided into true art, which is worthy of discussion, and popular culture, which is contemptible. In such a view, the only worth of the popular arts is that they give us something to shoot at, or at best, something from which to wean away the hoi polloi. I must confess that I share these views to an extent, for I remain convinced that there is more in Dostoevsky than in Dagwood, more in Holbein than in Hallmark Cards, more in Job than in James Bond. But this does not mean that there is nothing in Dagwood, Hallmark Cards, and James Bond. To take such a stand would be to deny the democratic sanction of popular arts, and I am unprepared to make such a denial. Faith in the democratic sanction I will admit to as a twentieth-century provincial. Its foundations are in the United States of America, its prophet being Thomas Jefferson, but the democratic sanction is both premise and goal for every civilized nation and people in the world today. We freely accept democracy and equality in political practice, and even when we observe the inherent hazards of democracy to excellence, to individuality, to creativity, to benevolent leadership, when a decision must be made, we will choose democracy as the more reliable alternative, and the more massive good.

But may we presume to accept the democratic sanction in politics but deny it in taste? This is a tough question, and it deserves some attempt at an answer. In part the answer lies in Jefferson's faith in the people

as the political norm, which was qualified by the requirements that
the people be literate, fully informed, universally educated, and
accustomed to self-government. The same requirements might be
imposed upon the acceptance of popular tastes as legitimate standard
for aesthetics. If the people are widely acquainted with the arts and
accustomed to selecting their cultural objects, their majority tastes
will be good. However, in neither politics nor in arts has the Jeffersonian ideal been satisfied in our world. Too many people choose from
alternatives in art or in politics from postures governed by ignorance,
whimsy, or perversity; and for many, both politically and aesthetically,
no alternatives are provided.

Whether or not there are alternative choices available to a people is
important to any investigation of popular arts. In a totalitarian society oftentimes the government will impose an aesthetic upon the people,
upon the artists, and upon the industries that convert the work of
artists into a mass product. Even where a strongly ideological government does not impose the aesthetic and the patterns for the arts, it
will surely discourage or restrict certain styles and products. One of
the best cases in point is that of Soviet opposition to American popular
music, but there are many others that surface from time to time in
periods of extreme nationalism. I speak here of officially imposed
aesthetic standards, however, not of the spontaneous popular opposition to some art or branch of art that relates to public policy. For
example, the anti-German hysteria in the United States during the
First World War that led to sauerkraut's being renamed "liberty cab-
bage" and German-fried potatoes being renamed "American fries"
also led to popular opposition to German music, but this was not so
much a matter of policy as it was a matter of mass opinion. Similarly,
public policies about obscenity and pornography may as often be
reflections of popular opinion as they are of ideological impositions.
The continuing ambiguity in respect to United States obscenity legislation is such a reflection of public uncertainty, just as Scandinavian
liberality may reflect popular assurance more than an official promulgation of the obscene arts.

I wish to expand upon this political analogy, because I think within
it lie some of the more important questions of popular aesthetics on an
international scale. Over the past several years I have discerned a
general but basic difference between North American and European

studies into mass popular arts. Among Europeans there seems to me to be a fear of popular arts and an urgent concern for the upraising of popular tastes. Among Americans there is an attitude that ranges from wry acceptance to uncritical affection for the popular arts. Any who have read the Journal of Popular Culture or who have attended any of its conferences must have observed that American students of popular culture never seem to ask whether or not popular culture is a "good thing." The reason for this, I think, is that popular culture is virtually all that there has ever been in America - popular culture or the wilderness - and the youthful rebels of the Sixties and Seventies who cried out against our dominant popular culture headed for the wilderness securely buttressed with the best-selling Whole Earth Catalog, which instructed them where to write for manufactured do-it-yourself supplies, the best-selling Stalking the Wild Asparagus of Euell Gibbons, which told them of the vitamin content of the foods they foraged in the wilderness, the best-selling novel In Watermelon Sugar of Richard Brautigan which substituted communal watermelon factories for capitalistic plastics plants.

The young rebels' tradition in America is well-founded. More than a century ago their forefathers rejected urban life and went to the wilderness with best-selling homesteaders' handbooks and Ralph Waldo Emerson's best-selling Self-Reliance. The point that I am making, however, is that in America popular culture has afforded people a rich variety from which to choose, and notwithstanding the attacks by young middle class Americans on popular culture, few have been denied alternatives within the culture. One alternative does not exist for Americans, though, the alternative of a traditional cultivated society without mass production and with a sense of place and long-term history. For Americans there is wilderness or popular culture, but no traditional social-cultural alternative. For that reason, Americans do not fear popular culture to the same degree as Europeans and Asiatics fear popular culture, because for the Americans there is no other culture on which to build.

I should not want it thought that there are no cultivated arts in our country. Far from it, but such art seems to be most effective where it draws upon either the wilderness or the popular arts. Consider Thomas Cole, William Cullen Bryant, Walt Whitman, George Caleb Bingham, Mark Twain, Charles Ives, John Dos Passos, John Steinbeck,

Aaron Copland, Leonard Bernstein, Roy Lichtenstein, Andy Warhol, Kurt Vonnegut, Andrew Wyeth - a mixed bag of artists, certainly, and chosen to avoid long debates about Hawthorne, Henry James, T. S. Eliot, Samuel Barber, Marianne Moore, and the like -, but nevertheless, the list should suggest that in both form and content, America's conscious artists often draw inspiration from landscape and mass culture rather than from a classic tradition, a social milieu, or a logical premise. These latter traditions, it seems to me, are the mainstreams of the European tradition founded upon Platonic dialogue rather than upon nature or popular culture. Specific instances will provide exceptions, but the general distinction will remain valid.

This rather lengthy aside is important because we must clearly distinguish an investigation of popular aesthetics from an investigation of ideological aesthetics. The kind of popular aesthetics of which I speak must be a product of a relatively open market where there can be a democratic sanction of arts, styles and artifacts. Therefore, to believe that there is something of value in Dagwood, Hallmark Cards, and James Bond is to imply faith in democracy of taste, or as I sometimes state it in the folksy idiom of Abraham Lincoln, God must have loved the popular artifact because He made so many of them.

You will notice that this statement does not deviate from the simple standard stated at the outset, that what sells is good art, what does not sell is bad art; but I would maintain that it is necessary that the people have a choice in what they buy and that the purveyors of popular arts be subject to competition. Thus, prior to the development of commercial television channels in Great Britain, it could not have been said that any knowledge of popular aesthetics could be derived directly from BBC television, regardless of how much television may be a mass medium of communication and entertainment. An even more dramatic instance of this is to be found in the off-shore "pirate" radio stations that offered to serve certain popular tastes in Great Britain during the Sixties.

The pirate radio stations are useful to my discussion of popular aesthetics for another reason, because it appears that popular aesthetic standards are always outlaw aesthetics, by which I mean that popular tastes will assert themselves regardless of how much they are opposed and repressed, how much the people are instructed, or how much they

are given an elevated aesthetic diet upon which to feed. A case in point is that of the comic book, for which there was no cultivated antecedent, for which there was no training in school systems any-where, and against which the greatest forces of education, criticism and morality were directed in every society that was subjected to the comics. The same outlaw characteristic marked dime novels, penny dreadfuls, music halls, early movies, jazz and rock music. This is not mere moral outlawry, which would be directed at a behavior-corrup-ting intent of popular arts; it is aesthetic outlawry that seems to be directed at the corruption of public tastes.

Can any generalizations be made about the outlaw characteristics of the popular arts, that is, generalizations that cut across the many modes of the arts? I think so, but I must warn that you will not be surprised by the general standards of popular arts. All successful popular art forms are clear and simple. When they lose clarity and simplicity, either one of two things will happen to them; they will die from lack of audience, or they will win a new, more cultivated, sophisticated and exclusive audience. But before I discuss that phenomenon, I would like to explain more fully how clarity and simplicity are the formal characteristics that are the universals of popular aesthetics.

In the visual arts, it is my observation that the popular audience does not take to shadows or gradations in color. For that reason, the popu-lar audience is far more attracted to Raphael than to Rembrandt, and while there is no end to the popularized and mass-produced progeny of Raphael's well-lighted and brightly colored scenes, there are few equivalent popularized outgrowths of Rembrandt's style. Similarly, the popular aesthetic requires clear distinction between visual ob-jects. It prefers a stated boundary, as in the early nineteenth-cen-tury cartoons of Rowlandson, to an implied one, as in the paintings of Turner, or as in Rex Morgan as opposed to Francis Bacon.

The same rule applies to the moving visual arts. The popular aes-thetic prefers Walt Disney's Bambi to his Fantasia and it prefers Cecil B. DeMille to Jean Cocteau. In the arts of man in motion, the popular aesthetic prefers the broadly sustained grace of Ice Capades to the momentary and ephemeral grace of ballet, or the unambiguous expres-sion of conflict in professional wrestling to that of dance. In the music of dance, the popular audience wants reliable meters, not counter-

9

rhythms, and the same thing is true of popular song. Furthermore, the popular aesthetic prefers music to be loud rather than soft. The popular audience wishes to hear things as clearly as it wants to see things. So far I have restricted myself to formal elements, but the same standards of clarity and simplicity apply to content. Good must be clearly distinguished from evil, strength from weakness, melancholy from joy, patriotism from treason. I need hardly provide examples of these.

It all seems so easy. But it is not quite so elementary as I have made it, at any rate, it is not so elementary if you share my faith in the democratic sanction, because the popular demands for clarity and simplicity are not to be regarded as reflections of simpleminded stupidity. The people are not fools or dupes; it is just that they want expression to be understandable. The expressive forms of popular arts, in other words, must be simple, but the underlying ideas, concepts and philosophies may be most profound, and of a complexity that transcends much cultivated discourse. Students of traditional folk culture are perfectly familiar with this apparent paradox, and are not fooled by the childishly broad forms of the collected folk tales of the brothers Grimm, nor by the quaint repetitions of the collected ballads of Bishop Percy. They do not confuse the angular abstractions of African sculpture with puerile primitivism. And neither do they assume that the stereotypes of the American western hero represent shallowness of understanding. All these folk forms - fairy tales, ballads, icons, and heroic fables are expressions of human longings, fears, despairs and dreams - simpler, cruder and briefer than the works of Sophocles, Aquinas, Rembrandt, and Strindberg, but no less expressive of the tragic state of the human condition.

It is my contention that the popular audience, if it is given a choice, will always tend toward the more profound meanings, so long as the aesthetic demands of simplicity and clarity of expression are not violated. Trivial and empty popular art works have the life expectancy of a glass of Coca-Cola; they must be consumed immediately or cast out or replenished. They will effectively satisfy the thirst of the moment, and none of us is immune to that. But the long-lasting popular art forms are for sustenance, something to which we must return to sustain our unexpressed, and often unconscious, needs and beliefs. That is one of the reasons that Americans so long have returned to the popular western. Every American, except for blacks

10

and Indians, bears the guilt of descent from some person who denied
and rejected traditional civilization. In part, the Western reenacts
the beginnings of that guilt, that wrenching away from civilized life
to hammer out a new civilization from the wilderness. The Western
is a rationale that says: we were not wrong, there is rightness in our
violent quarrel with wilderness, for out of it comes a new harmonious
civilization. This is a strange belief, some will say. It is strange,
and its incomplete reality requires continuous sustenance, and the
popular Western is one of the arts that sustains it.

The Western, however, is a popular art and myth that has been often
explained and defended. I would now like to touch upon another popular art form that is rarely defended, that of the teen-ager's popular
song. These are the bread-and-butter of the recording industry and to
a very large degree, of the popular radio station and the transistor
radio industry. The songs, be they rock, soul, ballad or novelty, are
nearly all about love. They are superficial, they are stereotyped,
shallow and ephemeral. But they exist, they sell, and their popularity
implies aesthetic rightness, if my dictum that good sales mean good
art is correct.

A common mistake about popular aesthetics is to insist upon universal
aesthetics for the popular audience. This is most unwise, for it leads
to criticism that tries to explain away popular teenage music by either
lamenting the erosion of popular tastes, or by exposing the bad art of
popular music. The aesthetic standard that I have presented should
clearly establish the fact that aesthetically this is good music, because
it sells. But it sells only to a narrow audience of girls and boys who
largely outgrow it by the age of seventeen. The popular art of teen-age
music satisfies vague, irrational needs that the cultivated adult establishment tries, always unsuccessfully, to satisfy with rational expressions of reassurances about the future, with charts, with textbooks,
with church socials, with women's liberation polemics. Unlike these
reassurances, teen music does not have the approval of parents and
other adults, but it does have the democratic sanction of those adoles-
cents who listen to it, because it satisfies their indefinable needs.

Critics of teen music also regard it as a signal of the dissolution of
standards for arts and morals in the twentieth century, for there is no
antecedent to this popular music. The latter point is partly true, be-

II

cause the teen-ager is the product of the modern world and of universal popular education. Teen-agers do not exist in non-technological
societies, but wherever mass industry and increased technology have
ended traditional agricultural life and family industry, and have increased the tenure of formal education, teen-agers have evolved, and
they have evolved without cultural provisions for the psychology and
physiology of post-pubescent celibacy and vocational inactivity. The
first nation to undergo the creation of a teen-age class was the first
industrial nation, England, and it was the first nation to see mass popular arts develop a means of serving the wants for which no traditions
were ready. The art form that developed was the novel, but we know
the popular feminine novel primarily by way of attacks of the adults,
who ranted about the immorality of novel-reading, or through serious
novelists, like George Eliot, who leveled one of her first pieces of
aesthetic criticism against "silly lady novelists." Only Jane Austen
seems to have been able to satirize the sentimental teen-age novel at
the same time that she understands and sympathizes with the teen-ager.

The teen-age girls' novel is still with us, although it is probably being
supplanted by teen music, but both of these art forms continue as outlaw arts, reviled and ridiculed by mature women and ignored by baffled
men, but going on with the sureness of an aesthetic that expresses
meanings quite as subtle as the cultivated arts.

The example of teen music is but one illustration of the subtlety and
complexity of the popular aesthetic and its responses to the myriad contingencies of the marketplace. Those who have worked with theatre
know that artistic expression is always limited by human contingencies.
The capacity of the human bladder sets restrictions on the length of a
performance; the acuteness of the human ear, on size of audience.
The limits of human vision set the effective borders on the scope of
theatre; the night perception of the human eye sets requirements of
the stage lighting. And the limits of the human brain restrict the number of ideas and information bits that can be comprehended simultaneously or at length.

Mass art forms share all these contingencies, but they must contend
with even more contingencies of a social and economic nature. One
of these is that many popular arts are directed at a mass audience
that are widely separated from one another and at a remote distance

from the artist. Frequently, it is made up of individual people who
are alone. And the artist cannot, like the folk storyteller or singer,
compensate for waning interest in an immediate audience, nor can he,
like the cultivated artist, confer with his patron in advance of the
program. Other limitations are imposed by economics. Popular music
on the radio, for example, must make room for frequent commercial
announcements. The loudness must be steady enough to be heard
easily in an automobile or a cafe. Popular books must accept some
limits on quality of paper, printing and bindings to make a large output feasible. Popular filmmakers must make a spectacular enough
film to woo audience from their television sets and newspapers.

These hardly exhaust the contingencies of popular aesthetics. They
exist in a complicated network that may spell the demise of a whole
popular art form. Consider the first of the great arts born of mass production, the long novel. Appreciation of the long novel of the nineteenth century requires time and close attention. Consequently, it
cannot win popularity by eye-straining flickering firelight, but it will
lose popularity in fluorescent light where the peripheral environment
is fully illuminated. Long novels are best read by lamplight, quiet,
steady and narrow lamplight. The same thing is true for long poetry.
By contrast, romantic lyric poetry reads well outside, close to the
natural referents of the verse. Novels, though, which recreate exotic
times, places and societies work best where the natural or domestic
periphery is subdued or obscured. Cinema requires the same obscure-
ness of the periphery, and as Eisenstein has told us, through technology,
the cinema can employ the same violations of the Aristotelean unities
as can the novel. In other words, the contingencies imposed on the
environment of the audience by technological and social changes may
have direct bearing on the births, lives and deaths of popular art forms.
The popular long novel has not declined because the popular audience
is seated in a new environment, and other art forms have developed
that are more appropriate to that newly situated audience.

It will be observed that most of these remarks about popular aesthetics
have had a social, economic and political tone that may seem opposed
to true aesthetics, which in our century tends toward art for art's
sake, and consequently, toward strictly formal analysis. There is
no reason to apologize for this social emphasis, indeed, I can think
of nothing more wrong-headed and even dishonest than to discuss any

13

popular art irrespective of audience, for it is the audience that makes it popular. Without denigrating higher aesthetics, I would even say that this is what the most abstract and abstruse of aestheticians is really doing: he is inquiring into the qualities that make a given artwork popular with cultivated audiences. Rarely will he employ any touchstones other than the most popular works of, for example, Shakespeare, Wagner, or Mondrian. It is the audience that makes the artist worthy of investigation.

I do not want to say, however, that formal analysis is entirely inappropriate to studies in the aesthetics of popular culture. Formal analysis is one of the disciplines that interdisciplinary criticism may draw upon, but it cannot be the only one. I might illustrate with some instances from this book. On video aesthetics, for example, I have found that the formal approach of artistic self-consistency within the medium works well, while in the chapter on the aesthetics of popular education, where I employ primers and first readers as examples, pure form is much less significant than straight historical development. On the question of athletic aesthetics, I found strict comparison with a cultivated art most useful, comparing wrestling and ballet. In popular religious art, I have used cross-cultural comparisons, as well as the more formal considerations of such things as the effects of the rotary press upon mass-produced cultivated art works. But in every case, the audience and the industry are of the greatest importance if we are to arrive at a more sensitive understanding of the aesthetics of popular culture. The audience, the industry, and the object, for while the audience may discern abstract values in popular arts, and the industry may try to express ideals, the object, be it book, film, wall decoration, or song is the medium that is bought, used up, cast away, or treasured.

Notably absent from consideration is the artist-creator, for in popular aesthetics, the artist is servant to the culture, or if you will, slave to the market. If his individuality asserts itself in style, innovation, leadership or complexity of philosophy and expression, we are in a different realm of aesthetic consideration, where the artist ceases to act as a tool for popular expression and becomes one who reforms and revises popular tastes, often to the degree that the popular audience abandons their former values of beauty. What was good art, no longer sells, and it ceases to be good art. Thus, we need not fear the mass

arts, for the true artist-reformer is possible in popular culture, sometimes as an outsider from the cultivated tradition, but sometimes, too,
as an insider who outgrew the simple, clear strictures of the popular
aesthetic. Such artists may win a cultivated audience, and they may
even lose their popularity in the process, and so new questions of
aesthetics will arise because of their uniqueness. From outlaws, these
artists are converted to in-laws, and we must inquire into this strange
misalliance, asking, for example, how is it that Jane Austen and
Louisa May Alcott rise out of the teenage sentimental novel? How
does Dickens rise from antecedents of William Harrison Ainsworth and
R. S. Surtees? How does George Gershwin rise from Tin-Pan Alley,
and Duke Ellington from dance-hall entertainment? How do we go
from Astounding Science Fiction to Kurt Vonnegut, from Hopalong
Cassidy to High Noon, from television serials to The Wives of Henry
VIII, from the early Beatles to Sergeant Pepper? The answer in every
case is in large part a matter of individual genius, but of genius that
originally responded to the expressive needs of many, many people by
building upon the assured appeals of the popular aesthetic, which says
an art work is good because it sells, and it sells because it never
places art above audience; rather fitting the form to the society, the
theatre to the living room, the book to the pocket, the car to the
driver, and the bottle to the hand.

15

The Limited Art of Popular Televisic

During the early years of television, magazine advertisements for television receivers depicted slim, elegantly dressed personages, tastefully deployed about a television set upon which was invariably to be found the image of a ballerina. With the advent of color television, the viewers remained about the same, but the danseuse now alternated with a brightly made up circus clown. The intended symbolism is obvious: the dancer represented culture and motion; the clown color and pageantry. Yet the symbolism unmasks the negative truth that the expressive scope of television is extremely limited. Neither ballet nor the circus can be successfully transposed into the video medium, because both ballet and circus are entertainment art forms that require that the audience be enveloped in a total experience, not in a tubular view of facial close-ups and miniscule long shots. The essence of ballet is to be found in the total composition of dancers' bodies within a three-dimensional stage, with light and sound waves invigorating a space shared by audience, dancers and dance. And the circus is all of this - with popcorn, sweat, smoke and dung besides. Thus, television cannot but fail in its attempts to express the arts of dance and of the three-ring world.

As a matter of fact, television has not only failed to transfer other
arts into its form, but television has almost completely failed to find
any expressive art form which is peculiarly its own. My recognition
of the lack of a genuine video aesthetic or experience started a few
years ago when my family and I lived in a cabin in the woods of
northern Minnesota. Our only source of electricity was a gas-powered
generator that wouldn't start when the temperature was below zero,
which was usually, and so we ordinarily had neither electic lights nor
television. But by our second year in the woods, we had discovered
that we preferred candles anyway, and we discovered too that one
rarely needed a television picture to enjoy television.

Some of our local television stations have audio bands that reach into
the FM radio portion of the electromagnetic spectrum, and so it became
our practice to sit by candlelight and listen to television programs on
our battery-operated radio. It made for very good radio. All of the
situation comedies turned out to be radio programs, even those television shows that seem to depend upon sight gags. For example, we
heard the first of the Get Smart series without a picture, and when a
few years later we saw reruns of those programs, we found that we had
accurately imagined almost everything except the faces. My son was
at the Saturday morning cartoon age at the time, and he enjoyed cartoons as old time radio shows, for most of the sound tracks were made
up of highly expressive sound effects, along with the voices of such
radio personalities as Ned Sparks, Clifton Finnegan, Senator Claghorn
and Gabriel Heatter. We also discovered that most mysteries and
dramas are auditory expressions, although western movies and the
finales of adventure films pose a problem, because the radio listener
only receives thundering hoofbeats, screaming tires – and chase music.

But there was among the television shows one newcomer that we were
unable to visualize. It was called Mission Impossible, and all that the
audio brought through to us was whirrings, clicks, long silences, and
occasional tough dialogues between people speaking the thoughts of
Juan Peron and John Foster Dulles in heavy Guatemalan-Hungarian
accents. Mission Impossible, in other words, was the only regular
television entertainment program that was artistically – that is, aesthetically – a truly video experience. It was not written as a radio
show, and neither was it filmed as a movie with Hollywood cinematic
long shots, panoramic sweeps and cluttered pageantry. Instead, it

employed close shots, slowly evolving mechanical processes, and
rapid cuts to sharply distinctive faces registering emotional and intellectual responses. Just as radio had developed a corral of distinctive
voices to compensate for its one-dimensionality, Mission Impossible
employed sharply differentiated faces for its regulars, at least in its
first years. Later, however, Mission Impossible retreated from the
aesthetic frontier, and the verbal exchanges among the totalitarian
Esperanti increased to the point of converting the series into a radio
program with pictures.

Of course there is nothing "wrong" about television programs that are
aesthetically radio; total aesthetic consistency is not required for one's
deriving enjoyment from television, or, for that matter, from any other
art form. People who enjoy Broadway musicals or symphony concerts
would be silly to reject phonograph recordings of music just because
the music is not where it "should be" performed, in a theatre or concert hall. Anyone is free to enjoy any art in any form he chooses,
for personal enjoyment is one legitimate standard for aesthetic judg-
ment; yet, this rationale puts Grandma's delight in the Sunday school
Christmas pageant into the same bag with George Bernard Shaw's
delight in Das Rheingold; that is, they both "liked the show." Thus,
while I am not questioning the right of anyone to enjoy and to approve
of television programs that are essentially radio programs or ones that
are wide-screen movies squished into a television screen, I am saying
that any medium or mode of artistic expression has characteristics that
make it unique, and that it is most effective when expression is consistent with the medium. This has long been one aesthetic standard
for judging art: to assess the appropriateness with which form and content are applied to a given medium. A poet who wants to tell an
adventurous story does not pick a sonnet as his expressive form; indeed,
today he is not likely even to choose a poem as his medium of expression. Not if he wants anyone to read his story.

And that brings up one more aesthetic standard, one of particular importance in popular arts such as television. This is the Nielsen rating
aesthetic, which is a standard that has always stood in the way of pure
art, the art that exists irrespective of audience. Pure art probably
does exist, but in reality almost every artist has to do something in the
attention-getting mode of Haydn's Surprise Symphony, if only to assure
himself of an audience, and the history of music since the Renaissance

has been full of what the music trade calls "New Sound," all the way from antiphonal singing and Beethoven's trombones, to Mahler's Symphony for a Thousand, which is about as far as attention-getting technique can go, at least in the mode of symphonic tonality. Mahler's Symphony is an instance of the stegosauri of art that mark the effective end of developmental line, when a mode of expression has been stretched to its limits. Television seems to have reached its expressive limits by 1970 in Mission Impossible, Laugh-In and Batman.

In its earliest days, commercial entertainment television was quite self-conscious about what it would be. It never considered itself to be radio; it was constantly admonished not to be cinema, and it felt it must be something more than a mere converter of circus and ballet; yet nearly all of its functions were these three: radio with pictures, film with an ill-focused miniscule screen, and converter of other entertainment forms. The one exception was the Chicago School-Playhouse 90 achievement, which was stage theatre, live, immediate, and with the viewpoint of Mr. Firstnighter looking at a stage with a circular proscenium. Something like a vertical theatre in the round.

Early television's uncertainty as to what it might be was a situation similar to that of the young Charles Dickens, who started The Pickwick Papers as a collection of short sketches in the mode of the day, competent but conventional, and not quite sure what he or it might be, until he found midstream that he should be writing a Dickens novel, which thereupon he did. The similarity of Dickens' technique and viewpoint to that of cinema had been noted by Sergei Eisenstein, and much of what Eisenstein wrote applies to video, but there is the additional similarity that Dickens operated under the same Nielsen rating aesthetic restriction as television. Television, like radio, was competing with movies , which used lavish extravagance to draw people from their homes; and television, like radio, and like Charles Dickens, adopted the technique of building an audience by means of weekly serial installments. Serial publication or broadcast places other restrictions on all three of these popular art forms, the double requirements of prescribed chapter length and a cliffhanger ending to bring the audience back next week. Part of Dickens' achievement that made his popular art into great art is that he preserved an overall unity throughout the serials, and that he created an artistic and dramatic inevitability that carries readers through the novels even today.

19

Serial radio never achieved this, and the closest parallel in American television was The Fugitive and its various spawn, such as Run For Your Life and The Invaders. But The Fugitive possessed the same weakness as a novel that should be a short story - the fugitive's weekly close calls contributed in no way toward the final episode, which contained the whole story. British television followed the practice of placing a hero in a situation that carries throughout infinite episodes with Patrick McGoohan's The Prisoner, but then, in The Forsythe Saga, the British took the lesson of the Victorian novel in toto; and finally, in such mini-series as The Wives of Henry VIII, produced unified, original video serial drama, with a beginning, a middle, and an end. The video success of Henry VIII can be affirmed by applying a simple aesthetic test: could it be effective as a one-sitting film, or as a radio program, or as a stage drama or as other theatrical form? The answer is "no" to all of these, and the reason is partly because of the Dickensian serial novel technique.

But that is only part of the explanation. The quest for a video aesthetic is not only a matter of how one holds the audience; it is also a matter of how one uses the television screen. This is a problem of artistry; the popular audience doesn't really care beyond wanting to see things clearly, and yet it is the audience that spurs the popular artist on to develop the potentials of the medium. The artist cannot ignore the simple demands of the audience, indeed, he must share them, and the audience responds to the artistic improvements by rejecting less sophisticated styles with the derogatory term "old-fashioned." It is, after all, the highly sophisticated audience that can watch old movies with interest; the popular audience wants only the latest thing. But while television was dealing with the initial problem of how to show a clear picture, cinema was asking other hard questions of art, for when commercial television began to force the closing of movie theatres in the early 1950's, filmmakers began to ask, what can theatre film do that television cannot, and what are the inherent limitations to both these media? The answers are implied in wide-screen cinemascope and stereophonic sound, for it was rightly concluded that the smallness of the television screen and the tinniness of the sound were the vulnerable limitations of the competition. But what this answer did not tell was how to use a wide screen and stereo sound. The first artistic attempts in the new form were The Robe and Shane, in 1953, the former using the screen for "casts of thousands,"

20

the latter, for photographing wide landscapes. These two practices
remain standard good uses of the medium, as, for example, in Dr.
Zhivago and Lawrence of Arabia.

Yet these boil down to "Same Thing, Only Bigger," and do not explain how to use the wide screen in interiors and close-ups. The total
use of wide-screen and stereophonic sound in American cinema had to
wait for the 1955 production of Jack Webb's Pete Kelly's Blues, which
opened with a view of a New Orleans funeral band marching across
the screen and across the audience consciousness, both visually and
aurally. Thematically the film is about jazz of the 1920's, and thus
the new sound system is an inherent part of the experience. Interior
scenes are staged to exploit the medium, as, for example, placing
Peggy Lee, in the role of schizoid ex-torchsinger, at the extreme end
of an expansive empty room in an insane asylum, pathetically isolated
from her interlocuter at the other end of the screen. An entirely different effect was produced in the film climax which was shot in a
cavernous empty dance hall, with a revolving mirror-studded ball
filling the screen and enveloping the audience in a firmament of scat-
tering lights, punctuated stereophonically with a crossfire of gunshots.
These are contrived devices that might explain why Pete Kelly's Blues
seems never to be included in art film programs, but, on the other hand,
film societies are usually tied to 16mm projection so that they are ill-
equipped for looking at a film that is aesthetically bonded to the wide
screen stereophonic sound media.

Applying the same sort of test as was given to Henry VIII, it is clear
that Pete Kelly's Blues is pure cinemascope expression, and could not
communicate the same experience in television, radio or narrow-
screen cinema. In other words, Jack Webb exploited the medium
instead of merely applying the proven techniques of other media. This
is notable in itself, but it is even more remarkable when it is remembered that Webb achieved the same kind of artistic success in television, in the Dragnet series. The very fact that Dragnet successfully
returned to television after a long recess, and that its video techniques
were extended without alteration to Adam-12 and other shows, points
up the effectiveness of the Webb television style, which is in polar
opposition to his Pete Kelly's Blues style. Webb's television series
are essentially radio shows (both Dragnet and Pete Kelly's Blues
started as radio drama), containing almost nothing that is indispen-

21

sably visual. But unlike most television programs that were contemporaries of early Dragnet, they did not attempt to crowd film or stage perspectives into a television screen. Rather, they gave the popular viewer what he wanted, a clear, easy-to-see unambiguous picture. Jack Webb exploited the television medium within its severe limitations, just as he was to do later with the very different limitations of cinemascope.

The inherent limitations of television as an art form are myriad. The screen is small, virtually square in shape. The image does not allow for fine detail, nor for nuance in shading. These factors combine to make of television a two-dimensional medium. It is difficult to create an image that can draw a viewer into a background or to surround him with a panorama. Not only is the screen incapable of creating the illusion of space in depth, but it cannot create lateral space either, at least not without reducing significant objects to a few insignificant electronic dots. In addition to this, the television camera cannot sweep over a scene or record rapid motion. The Dragnet answer to these restrictions, as everyone knows, is staccato dialogue with staccato facial shots, interposed with closeups of telephones ringing, car doors opening, doorbells being pressed, and all the other visual irrelevancies that Webb inherited from Alfred Hitchcock. But such closeups are, in primitive form, the same techniques that were to be refined and used to tell a story visually in Mission Impossible.

Ironically, for a time cinemascope filmmakers borrowed these techniques from television with the result that theatre audiences had to accustom themselves to being enveloped in Brobdignagian cleavages and in dinosauric close-ups of actors' pores and pimples. The close-up problem of wide-screen cinema has only recently been solved by such devices as are employed in Andromeda Strain to mask out and to divide the screen into appropriate smaller areas.

Between Dragnet and 1970, however, television directors and cameramen experimented and found new techniques to compensate for the two-dimensional restrictions of television. First was the use of unusual camera angles that either create such extreme foreshortening that the viewer is forced to accept the existence of a third dimension (overhead shots of people conversing, for example); or shots that place an actor, who stands in middle distance, beyond the frame of a close-

22

up vase, or a chair bottom, or, in the extreme of video pixiness, from inside Frank Nitti's wall safe in The Untouchables. For a truly aesthetic use of these video techniques, The Untouchables was probably the most effective serial drama until Mission Impossible. In addition to using the Dragnet camera techniques, which deal with the third dimension by ignoring it; and in addition to using unusual camera angles and brilliant framing to evoke the third dimension, The Untouchables conquered the television screen's inability to show subtle shading by surrendering, and using instead contrasty chiaroscuro and dramatic sidelighting. Sometimes it was a little hard to see where anyone was, it is true, but eventually and invariably a beer truck would arrive upon the scene to lend a caravagian headlight. In spite of the arty camera effects and the beautiful exploitation of the television screen, however, The Untouchables was a radio program, even to its heavy reliance on Walter Winchell's voice as narrator, and the brilliant character actors who played the villains - Harold J. Stone, Victor Buono, Harry Morgan, Nehemiah Persoff, and Bruce Gordon - all men with voices as distinctive as their faces.

Another camera technique was borrowed by television drama from its own medium. Television sportscasting, of course, suffered the same ills that afflicted theatrical television, but the zoom lens came to the rescue, and a zoom-boom hit the viewer in the eye with such unnatural effects as that of suggesting that the human eye picks out an object in a distant scene by zooming in 10:1. Used excessively, this is as disconcerting as would be any sixty-minute trombone concert, but used judiciously, the zoom effect does evoke the third dimension.

More recent among television's overcompensations is the use of audio transitions to shift from one video scene to another. The most extreme form of this is the device of employing a close-up microphone to record conversations of people, in automobiles, in the distance, as they move from set to set. This is honest in its way; very few shots in filmmaking are made on location, and for very practical reasons. However, on television, this frank admission of what is ordinarily hidden technique, carries along with it an implied frank admission that video is often irrelevant. Because the video dramas are so largely radio dramas, the close-up sound track only serves to emphasize that most visual elements are only used as padding. This is illustrated in many series, but the short-lived detective series, Longstreet, may have led the field. The device is

not new; Buck Rogers comic strips in 1929 showed Buck and Wilma
speaking in "audio balloons" issuing at full volume from distant rocket
ships.

This may seem trivial, yet the artistic issue here is greater than one
viewer's feeling of irritability at an artificial technique. Art, after
all, is artifice. It is not "real," although art may depict, or represent, or interpret reality. And in so doing, any art form can choose the
course of verisimilitude, that is, the imitation of reality; or, it can
choose the course of stylization. If verisimilitude is the course taken,
artifice must be disguised. There are degrees of artifice, of course,
but no stage drama has been helped by letting the audience see that
the canvas "walls" flutter when a prop door is closed. Television
serial drama, like Hollywood cinema, tends toward verisimilitude
rather than stylization. Popular audiences, after all, prefer the familiar, and in modern society, mundane reality is familiar. But verisimilitude requires that the art always keep its guard up, so that its
techniques of artifice never obtrude into the viewer's consciousness.

Stylized theatre has similar demands for consistency, of course, but
stylized art is built upon suspended disbelief and upon the audience's
projected imaginations; verisimilitudinous art is built upon belief and
not upon devices that strain the audience's imaginations. Thus, television played a game of chance when it tipped its hand in Longstreet,
Macmillan and Wife and other serials to bring its own realism into
question. By contrast, Hollywood cinema, which thrived on imitation
of reality, even in its animated cartoons never revealed that almost
all voice-track was dubbed in. Television, it seems, was once more
pushing its expression beyond its own limitations as a popular art form.

My remarks up to now apply particularly to monochromatic television.
Color was expected to add a new dimension to the medium. Most
viewers will remember the anticipation of color as the panacea for
television's shallow aesthetics. Walt Disney ushered in regular color
programming, as he had contributed to early color cinema, yet his
success in both cases resulted from the use of flat primary colors of
simply structured two-dimensional figures. But beyond the use of
color for animation, there is little to be said for color television as
an artistic medium. The overall effect of television color on the
audience is about the same as it has been in cinema; it causes the

24

first minutes of any black-and-white program that follows to pale, and it makes the scenery the star. Consequently, the great moments of color television are not to be found in human drama, which knows no color prejudice, but in the science and nature films of Disney's Real Life Adventures, of National Geographic specials, of Jacques Cousteau's Underwater Worlds, of Bronowski's Ascent of Man. Aside from these and aside from color animations, color television's artistic effects have been limited to variations of programs of garishly caparisoned newscasters set against a background of flamboyant weather maps. As one variation of this technique, Laugh-In may have been the visual peak of color television human entertainment.

There is one other effect of color television that most viewers are quick to ignore. This is the compromise that the eye makes between the television spectrum and the natural spectrum. Excepting where the television people have deliberately reduced the studio spectrum to flat primaries, television color cannot hold a candle to movie color. There is nothing dishonest in this visual compromise - after all, we totally ignore the blueness of "black-and-white" - but aesthetically, it permits little nuance.

The limitations of television as an expressive medium, possessing its own aesthetic, appear to have been exploited to the extreme. Most television drama is either radio (with pictures added), or movies (with bad focus, color and scope). With few exceptions, the attempts to make the best of the limitations of the medium have produced frenzied camera effects, with concertina zooms, fanciful angles, freeze frames and garish color schemes. Put all of these together, and the logical outcome is Batman. Batman is worthy of further commentary, not because of its cute and obvious burlesques of comics and television, but because the program's term "guest villain" provides a key to understanding the characteristics of popular aesthetics. The "guest villain" is the differentiating factor not only in Batman drama, but in Mannix, Peter Gunn, and Dragnet; in Johnny Dollar, The Lone Ranger, and The Shadow; in Dick Tracy and Superman; and in The Perils of Pauline. In short, the overall aesthetic of television drama is a serial aesthetic, and this designation places most television drama into the same category as serial radio, serial comics and serial films. All of these depend upon the guest villain, whose office is that of providing a fresh problem for a resident staff of heroes to solve. Ultimately,

the serial aesthetic is the product of serial printing, and, while I suppose that we could trace it back through Dickens and Sir Roger de Coverly, I think it more likely that the serial aesthetic, as it operates in television, starts with the development of the hero and sidekick pattern: Tom Swift's Ned Newton and Eradicate Jones; Sherlock Holmes' Watson, Lestrade and Mrs. Hudson. The possible examples are countless, but it is clear that successful serial drama demands a little society of set characters whose Good Life would be a deathless Eden, were it not for the guest villains. Any serial that does not create a little permanent society is in danger of losing a popular audience. It is true, however, that Horatio Alger, Kathleen Norris, Zane Grey and other popular book authors succeeded in varying the characters, but they could not vary the types. Furthermore, theirs is not serial literature in the same sense that the Rover Boys, Nancy Drew, Tugboat Annie and Jeeves are serial.

P. G. Wodehouse's Jeeves exists in the slightly different genre of literary situation comedy, which is different from "serious" drama in that it does not require a guest villain. The antecedent for serial comedy is commedia dell'arte, and the reason that comedy does not require a guest villain is inherent to the little societies of commedia. Unlike the hero and sidekick pattern, which permits to the little society only comradeship and sycophancy, the commedia pattern is composed of a set of humour characters who are designed to conflict rather than to cooperate, and thus a guest villain is not needed, although an outside irritant may be used to trigger the humour conflicts. Therefore, Dick Van Dyke, The Honeymooners, Andy Griffith, Lucy and other situation comedies offer viewers the tantalizing security of continuous intramural conflict. This, then, is the serial aesthetic (comic sub-group). Given this analysis, some of the most popular television shows are explainable. Gunsmoke, for example, has a hero with a commedia group-sidekick, and various other series have succeeded with similar blends of the two modes: Bonanza, Ironside and I Spy are but three.

The serial aesthetic is not peculiar to television, but it is nevertheless the aesthetic glue that binds television to the other popular and mass arts, and it is the aesthetic barrier that stands between television and high art. The adherence of television to the serial format is also the main reason that video art, as an art in itself, has been

26

ignored, or disdained, or, more often, has been confused with its
aesthetic in-laws - theatre, film, and radio. As is so often the case
while a popular medium is developing important techniques, the cultivated critics keep looking for the techniques of established art forms
in the popular medium. This, I suspect, is what is behind the critical
acclaim awarded the early "Chicago School" live drama: it was theatre, and theatre critics applauded.

Serial art, of course, has achieved great moments in television, but
the great moments get lost in the series, and are almost irretrievable
when the series dies, or when the series is rerun in toto. The truth of
this, and the likelihood that television series will be lost can be demonstrated by reference to radio drama. Almost none of radio's theatre
has gone into repertory as art, except for the Orson Welles broadcast
adaptation of H. G. Wells' The War of the Worlds, and this, of
course, was not part of a series. But the power of Welles' famous
"scare" broadcast derives from a technique that underscores the essential nature of all mass media, which is that their most consistent
virtue is immediacy. The War of the Worlds was stylistically a news
broadcast, with "on-the-spot interviews" and "fast-breaking bulle-
tins." In short, the artistry was consistent with the traditions of the
medium rather than being built upon a superimposed outside aesthetic
drawn from stage, screen or literature. Thus, it would appear that
much of the best art of the "immediate media" is that which employs
the customary usages of the media, which are to receive news and to
alert the audience to happenings as they take place. This "news"
characteristic alone explains much of the transitory value of programming on radio and television.

Immediacy, therefore, is both a blessing and a curse, and above all,
it is a requisite for the effective use of the media for popular arts.
For the popular media arts, immediacy or the illusion of immediacy
must be communicated, and this is effected by the use of live and
canned audiences, and by the use of realism in preference to
expressionism or unbridled fantasy. Science fiction is realistic fantasy depending upon believable technologies, and thus in its very
reality, it is vulnerable to becoming out-dated as real space exploration, for example, changes public sophistication about planets and
interplanetary hardware. Still, immediacy continued to be the watch-
word in the non-theatrical popular radio that replaced dramatic comedy

and variety shows after the coming of television. Open-access telephone programs will come to mind as examples of immediacy, as well as disc jockeys' references to local events, weather and personalities. One of the extreme demonstrations of the importance of immediacy I observed in the operation of a computerized FM radio station in a small town in Arkansas in the late Sixties. Here, once each month, a professional announcer from Memphis would record a series of time and temperature "spots," with such immediacies as: "Well, folks, looking past my coffee pot bubbling here, I see we've got a bit of a shower outside, so you'd better make sure that Dad takes his umbrella. . . ." These warm remarks, then, were placed into the tape carousel to be played whenever the time and weather made them relevant. Series drama, too, insists upon immediacy. In some of the most popular of television and radio drama, the soap operas, immediacy is augmented by making the time and the place for the domestic situations as close as possible to that of the listening audience. Most "soaps" take place on television as they did in radio, in kitchens, dining rooms, and living rooms, during the daytime, thus providing a most scrupulous Aristotelean unity of time and place.

Of the radio soap operas, only one seems to be guaranteed the immortality which it deserves, partly because its scripts are preserved in the Wisconsin State Historical Society. But that is only a small part of the reason for the lasting value of Paul Rhymer's Vic and Sade, because Rhymer rejected the transitory characteristics of the serial art form at the same time that he exploited the immediate characteristics of the radio medium. The scripts were individual stories, and thus were not condemned to extinction from being fractured segments of an endless plot. Moreover, the settings were all in "the small house halfway up in the next block," and the time of action was almost always in the quiet part of the afternoon when the playlets were aired. Vic and Sade's contacts with the outside world were similar to those of the audience, in their small houses halfway up in the next block. Sadie Gook and her family learned of the events of the town from looking out the window, from sitting on the porch, from talking on the telephone, and from talking to one another. This last technique – the use of dialogue rather than narration for plot development – was shared with all daytime drama, but in Paul Rhymer's hands, dialogue and words were stylized into an audio experience, not remaining a mere mode of communication as in the other "soaps." Although the

28

words were delivered in a tone that was as flat as the Illinois-Indiana prairie on which the words were spoken, the dialogue was pungent in imagery and phrasing, and it was rhythmic by way of repetition of tart phrases, quiet malapropisms and outrageous names: Blue-Tooth Johnson, Smelly Clark, and Mr. Razorscum among them. Indeed, the only exceptional characteristic of these dramas was the language; the dramatic situations were unexceptional, the four characters were unexceptional, but the language - the audio-texture - was exceptional. And therein lies the potential permanence of popular media art, for the immediate must be given style, structure and universal truth (no matter how humdrum the universal may be), if it is to live beyond the moment.

It would be wrong to overstate the instance of Vic and Sade's permanent value, however, or to insist that The War of the Worlds might be the forerunner of radio-art societies. These radio examples do, nonetheless, suggest that survival of media art is the result of the artistic exploitation of the medium within its technical limitations, as well as suggesting that serial plots are subject to early deaths. Returning to television, possibly cassette television will produce a television equivalent to art film societies, and some of the great series shows will go into repertory.

But I doubt it. I do, though, have some candidates, as I am sure everyone does. For example, Boris Karloff's greatest performance is buried in an I Spy episode, where the aging Karloff plays the part of a contemporary Don Quixote. Many of the Combat episodes are profound instances of existentialism, filmed with beautiful camera work. Somewhere in the Checkmate files is a Charles Laughton-Sebastian Cabot master duel; somewhere in Mannix is an episode wherein Mike Connors and Victor Jory raised a detective series to the level of profound drama of father-son relationships. But these, like many other episodes, are victims of the serial art form. They are individuals lost in stereotype and in popularity, and they do not have the possibility of redemption that was built into Charles Dickens' serials, that is, a consciously wrought total structure. No, television is caught in the aesthetic of the comic strip.

This is a bleak pronouncement, but the effective truth of popular television's having reached its limits was borne out by the return of

29

Dragnet, after several years off the air, by the retreat of Mission Impossible from the video style it once had, by the loss of television audiences to the reborn movie theatres in downtowns and shopping centers all over the country, and by the intense interest young people are exhibiting in older films and old radio programming. For middle aged people, listening to golden age radio recordings can be explained as nostalgia, but for the generation that has grown up on television, radio and film represent mind-stretching new media of expression.

Does this mean that television has run its course? Far from it. But it has carried video expression as far as it is likely to go. The techniques have been tried that can be used for highly characteristic creative expression, and particularly if they are not tied to the endless series that operate in response to the Nielsen aesthetic, they can be as effective as the Henry VIII mini-series. The television commercial techniques have only been applied to a children's educational program, Sesame Street, and still await an artist to employ them in expressive adult entertainment. There are video frontiers beyond Henry VIII and Mission Impossible, but they are most likely to build upon the techniques already developed, to use them as a video aesthetic vocabulary. But television will also have to be recognized as having as its main quality what its name means: to see far away. The medium is the message, for television is not so much a medium for expression as it is an im-mediate extension of the sense of sight. Consider what have been the great moments in television. Early live drama. The 1952 Democratic Convention. The events following the assassination of President Kennedy. The Viet Nam War. The moon walk. The Watergate Hearings. There have been many others, but all of them share the characteristic of immediacy, the feeling that "you are there." And as an entertainment medium, television's prime function has again been that of distant seeing, of bringing into our homes movies, sporting events, drama - and ballet and circuses - never equalling the real thing, it is true, but always achieving a closeness and intimacy that no other medium can match.

Ballet, Boxing, Bullfighting

and other Sports

For many of us who have considered the question, "How can one tell what is 'good in the arts,'" the answers often result from the easy practice of arranging personal tastes so that they will correspond to the testaments of established authority. This adjustment of personal taste to agree with outside authority is, to a large degree, what school survey courses in the various arts are designed to do; yet the "master-works-historical survey" provides few tools for dealing with contemporary arts other than simply dismissing them as "bad," or at least, as not in the syllabus. Yet, today, art works and art forms from all national cultures, past and present, surround us in their original states and in copies. This is further complicated by the parallel existence of three lively traditions, the folk, the popular and the cultivated.

It is a bewildering cultural world, and growing more so, as an increasing variety of choices are made available to a widening audience of consumers. The problem is not only an individual matter. It is one of concern to tastemakers of all kinds, including critics, interpreters and teachers, who are confronted by patrons whose cultural experience is ordinarily restricted on the one hand to some establishment-sanctioned masterworks in school, and on the other hand to a very narrow exposure to popular arts in the open market. Yet all these persons can legitimately ask the question: "How do I know what is 'good' in the arts?"

Toward answering this question in a contemporary setting, we might examine some cultivated art traditions in relation to similar popular art traditions, to determine whether there are any characteristics inherent to cultivated traditions that justify raising them to the higher level of human value that they conventionally occupy.

The term art will develop shape and definition as the chapter progresses, but for the moment it may be most convenient to understand art as a neutral term, more closely related to artifice and to designed actions of any kind, than to customary aesthetic forms. Within the bounds of this permissive definition, we may consider as arts all forms of athletics, most particularly ballet and professional wrestling, which tend to be the most theatrical variants of their art categories. In colleges, it is quite as likely that one will find dance in a physical education department as a fine arts department. And professional wrestling is particularly directed toward an audience response, as are all theatrical forms. Audience response is worth examining, because the aesthetic experience is a two-way street, and the audience can be quite as important as the work of art. Indeed, in some areas of popular arts, it is the audience's response that identifies a cultural phenomenon as a work of art. That is, while sometimes the response of an audience is totally detached so that it is clear that the phenomenon is regarded simply as an event, and not as a work designed to produce an experience for the beholders, at other times a mere event can become an experience. This sort of distinction is not necessary in ordinary criticism of the cultivated arts, because the intention of all such art is to produce an aesthetic response in the audience and the event is pre-defined as an artistic experience; but in popular culture, many phenomena are not intended to be art, although they may be taken that way by the audience. For instance, athletic contests are intended to produce an outcome of win, lose, or draw, and not to produce a planned aesthetic response in the audience, yet oftentimes an audience-response is an incidental outcome of the contest, sometimes to the degree that the audience-response can convert a type of athletic contest into an aesthetic experience.

This is a simple enough thesis, but in reality it is not so simple. To illustrate the actual complexity of attitudes in athletics audiences, let me describe a contract session with the New York State Boxing Commissioner that was reported on national television late in 1970. The onlookers at the session crowded before the camera like disciples posing for the Last Supper, but they were delighted with the thick-tongued but sharp-witted verbal contest between Muhammad Ali and Joe Frazier. Clearly, the witnesses were an audience to a light entertainment, pleased with the aptness, quickness and imagery of the repartee. Their facial expressions showed that they did not confuse the artistic exchange of words with the physical match which was to follow, nor did they confuse it with the hard business-dealing that they were witnessing.

This type of civilized detachment is characteristic of many participants and spectators in professional athletics who derive enjoyment from skillful play -- physical and verbal alike -- rather than from mortal conflict. This attitude is what marks the boxing aficionado, who can take equal pleasure in a fifteen-round match decided on points as he can in another match that ends in a kayo in the third round. Athletic aestheticians are a minority, of course, and most fans invest more than their minds in sports. For most, sporting events fulfill more primal human needs, needs of cathartic experience, of displacement experience, of phenomenological experience, of mythic experience.

Today's professional boxing probably occupies a middle ground between the poles of civilized and primitive participation. On the civilized side, it is highly structured, with an elaborate code of legal and medical sanctions and restrictions, and also it is highly stylized with rules of good behavior and (in part) an elite audience which concerns itself with timing, pacing, strategy and grace of movement. This is an audience similar in sensitivity and sophistication (though not always in urbanity and cultural scope) to those who are patrons of opera, painting and the dance. But on the primitive side, boxing is certainly basic, for nothing could be much more direct than watching two human beings in the act of punching each other, no matter how much the primal conflict has been modified by a chivalric set of rules. The physical conflict is the only meaning inherent to boxing, and, thus, while boxing has rules, traditions and

technique, it has virtually no content.

Wrestling is another matter. Collegiate and Olympic wrestling, of course, are like the "best" boxing and are technical contests with no intrinsic meaning whatsoever; but professional wrestling is a mythic experience in which the audience participates totally in meanings. Whereas the audience to a technical sport are spectators, the audience to a mythic sport are participants. This difference may seem strange, because professional wrestling in America is known by everyone to be a most unreal sort of combat. Wrestling is fiction, boxing is fact. Wrestling is myth, boxing is reality. But there is a paradox here, for as Mircea Eliade has said of the native audiences of primal myth, "everything that myths relate concerns them directly." It is this direct concern which ties popular professional wrestling to the higher art forms of humanity, for the issues are not merely technical. They are real concerns about reality.

The degree of concern of the audience-participants can be demonstrated in a situation that affords an interesting contrast to the Joe Frazier–Muhammad Ali scene. In November of 1957, thirteen thousand fans poured into Madison Square Garden to witness an "Australian tag" match involving Antonino Rocca, "The Bruiser" Afflis, "Dr." Jerry Graham and Edouard Carpentier. The match proceeded with well-rehearsed brutality until Mr. Rocca noticed that the "Dr." had drawn real blood from him. Rocca retaliated, and as a Life writer reported, "up to this point the audience had been lively, throwing paper cups into the ring, but not abnormally demonstrative. Now, stimulated by what was probably the first honest competition they had ever seen, some hundreds surged forward toward the ring." The other wrestlers were somewhat taken aback, but eventually all four of them were drawn into the melee. A cohort of New York City police restored order, and eventually the four wrestlers were fined heavily for having importunely crossed the line between art and life. That dividing line is very important to the popular mind.

The significant thing here is that the spectators broke the ritual line between the audience and the performers when they recognized that the blood was real blood (not the encapsulated artificial blood that wrestlers often conceal in their mouths or hands), and when they recognized that the conflict was real, not rehearsed. In other words, the action of the spectators reveals that until reality obtruded into

34

the drama, they had been responding in an atmosphere of appropriately suspended disbelief.

What produced such violent participation among the spectators? Was it unwillingness to set the disbelief they had so willingly suspended firmly down on the ground again? To do so would be to reduce myth to athletics, to change ritual drama to sport. The _Life_ report does not tell us whether or not the mob's spleen was directed only at "Dr." Jerry Graham, who presumably had become a genuine villain. Even if this were the case, and the mob was reacting in defense of the injured wrestler, we must remember that this was a wrestling match, filled all along with brutally secreted blood, sweat and tears. No, the outrage was committed against art, not against a professional wrestler. Outside reality cannot be injected into an art form of any kind without offense. What if a ballet dancer, just notified that she had won the New York State Lottery, _really_ began to dance for joy in _Les Sylphides_?

There is reality, and then, again, there is _reality_.

The reality of myth and art is not superficial, nor is it mundane, nor is it temporal. It is eternal. In professional wrestling, the reality is the conflict between the powers of Evil and the powers of Goodness. This is a simple conflict when stated in dualistic terms, but in professional wrestling it is couched in an ambivalent ritual, if for no other reason than that Good cannot always triumph, because there would be no vocational future for an Evil wrestler who is a confirmed loser. This is not a problem in the similar mythic form of the Western novel or movie, because new environments and an infinite cast of villains can be recostumed in new personae. But in Westerns and wrestling, our interest is engaged not by realistic details, but by mythic reality, which is a reenactment of an eternal cultural truth: Evil opposes Good, and Good will triumph, but it is a long struggle. Between these two genres of popular myth, wrestling is more primitive in form, but, despite this, it is least simple in meaning. The primitive characteristics are obvious: near-naked bodies, stripped-down environment, two or four contestants, direct confrontation. The human meanings of the conflict between Good and Evil in wrestling are ambivalent, though, because villainy in wrestling, as in life, is a relative thing, and we cannot always determine by prior defi-

nition who is the villain, for when two children of Evil are matched -- let us say in today's midwestern wrestling circuit, "The Crusher" and "Dr. X" -- one wrestler becomes unmitigated in his evil, the other relatively good. It is much closer to human reality than is the invariable triumph of the cowboy hero over outlaws in mythic westerns. Furthermore, Evil will win the wrestling match as often as will Good, even though Good always wins a moral victory, for when Good is defeated, it is because he has fought fairly -- or at least relatively fairly.

There is another mythic reality to wrestling which the Western never allows. This is the rematch, which implies a cyclical view of life, much closer to non-western philosophies than the Hellenic-Judaeic structure of beginning, middle and end, which marks our literary and cinematic myths, where, when the town is "cleaned up," it presumably stays cleaned up.

The wrestling match is therefore more of a dialectic than a classical unit. It has an existential continuity. Each match is a slice-of-life, and the conflict sometimes is planned to spill over the temporal boundaries of the scheduled match, and of the spatial boundaries of the ring, so that the contestants often throw in a few blows before and after the bell, and almost as often throw out one another to continue fighting outside the ropes. Life as it is depicted in professional wrestling is not neatly bounded by bells and ropes. This, incidentally, is one of the many characteristics which divides wrestling from the other athletic contests. Boxing, as we have seen, must keep the conflict within bounds, and any theatrical conflicts are discrete from the match, as in the verbal exchange between Muhammad Ali and Joe Frazier. Basketball and football and hockey are likewise controlled by structural conventions, and whenever a player's personality goes out of bounds, the audience response is like that of the wrestling crowd at Madison Square Garden. They are offended by the violation of the boundaries of reality, and they react in reality, not in the conventional forms of audience-participation in the drama, such as paper-cup throwing at wrestling matches or cheering and chanting at team sports.

Also, team sports are not so humanistic and mythic as wrestling. The conflict in team sports is civil conflict, not a conflict in values; it

is we and they, not Good and Evil. There is no individual catharsis in social and civic team conflicts, and there are no ambiguities to strain the moral sense, for the spectators (when not technical aficionados) are reduced to mass beings.

In wrestling, however, even though the spectators are part of a mass, they act as a mass only when the individual conscience has been outraged by one wrestling performer or another. Most spectators of team sports, like most members of political parties, do not shift loyalties. For them, injustice is a matter of definition, not of individual decision. My team, right or wrong. The team-sport fan's morals are like those of Clevinger in Catch-22 who defines those who shoot at him as "the enemy" and never has to ask himself Yossarian's question, "Why are they trying to kill me?" There are no individual values here, only mass values dictated by the local super-ego.

But if all the above is true about professional wrestling, why is it that the sport has no intellectual high-brow following? If wrestling bouts truly embody profound mythic meanings and represent eternal human conflicts, and, if wrestling really is a theatrical expressive form and not a mere athletic contest, why is there no body of criticism about wrestling? The answer is clear. Professional wrestling is an enactment of brutal and savage confrontation which is repulsive to civilized sensibilities. Going deeper, it may be that the more highly educated person fears participation in the brutality of conflict. Educated spectators of wrestling take pains to point out to others that they are aware of the phoniness of the conflict, and there is not a "serious" sports commentator who doesn't put on an exaggerated knowing smile when he talks of the "artists of the grunt and groan." Such disclaimers are unique in criticism, because, for example, no one takes pains during a ballet to tell his neighbor that he knows that Giselle is not really dead; nor are sports commentators openly skeptical about baseball batters' idiosyncratic posturings. Only wrestling merits from spectators an announcement of superciliousness to clothe our animal instincts, as fashion clothes our animal bodies. Wrestling, like rape and murder, is too direct, too individual a form of violence. Civilized men prefer civic violence, like hockey and war. There, as participants, we may clothe ourselves in uniforms; there, as spectators, we may disguise ourselves in a cloak of amorality, and be aficionados who concern

ourselves with kill-ratios and league standings, instead of anguish and pain and right and wrong.

The above may be the deep-seated reasons for the cultured person's lack of interest in wrestling, but there are other reasons. For one thing, wrestling is crude. There is no grace of movement, no sense of design in professional wrestling. Secondly, the conflict is limited in scope. There is just so much which can be said about the human condition in a simple acting out of Good versus Evil. Because of its dramatic content, wrestling does have greater human meaning for audiences than other sports; yet, on the surface, it shares with all athletic contests the common simplistic outcome: victory, defeat or draw. It is true, of course, that in sports events individual players or teams will sometimes embody ancillary conflicts that bring some or all of the spectators into a human drama, as when an athlete makes a comeback after injury or illness, or a boxer is carrying to fruition a father's dream, or an underdog small-town basketball team wins the state tournament, or a member of a minority group makes the break-through into the Big Time; but these are incidental to the art form, much as grandma's appreciation of the Christmas play may derive entirely from her grandchild's involvement in the pageant. But to return to the reasons for the limited "serious" interest in professional wrestling, it is not only the case that wrestling is brutal and graceless, but it makes very shallow demands upon the imagination. No wider horizons are opened to the imagination from the conflict, and there are a limited number of holds that can be shuffled and redistributed and no new meanings will evolve from these. Wrestling is a dead-end form of theatre, yet of the popular spectator sports, professional wrestling is closest to the customary arts, just as dance is the cultivated art form closest to athletics. But before considering dance as an athletic art form, a summary of the foregoing may be desirable.

First, although all athletic events share a common purpose of producing a winner in a conventionalized contest, some contests have a further purpose of producing an aesthetic experience for the spectators. Professional wrestling, however, is probably the only contest in which the significance of audience experience totally supplants the importance of the outcome of the contest. This characteristic places wrestling closer to the arts than other sports, at

least in respect to content. Secondly, all athletic contests have some portion of the audience whose responses convert the essential contest into an art form. For these aficionados, the outcome is of less importance than the technique, and most particularly in Olympic contests, they are concerned with the beauty of physical movement and the strategic perfection of the contest. Theirs is an aesthetic attitude, but because the athletic contests have no expressive or theatrical purpose, the scope of the aficionados' responses are restricted to technical appreciation. Third, in addition to these technical appreciators of athletic events, there are often spectators who will invest a contest with extrinsic meanings, such as civic or national rivalries, or concern with the personalities of the participants. These extrinsic meanings, however, are accidents of the moment, and they do not make contests into art forms.

Dance, which is always accepted as a legitimate art form, possesses some notable similarities to wrestling. Both are rehearsed, both serve as vehicles for human meanings, both have dramatic structure. Wrestling and dance share another characteristic of being bodily forms of expression. Wrestling is probably the oldest of expressive art forms. In both there is a continuous and parallel folk tradition, all the way from spontaneous physical conflict in wrestling and purely emotional "dancing for joy" in dance, to the more specialized traditional variants, such as arm-wrestling and step-dancing. Both wrestling and dance have broad bases of highly developed ethnic forms to draw upon, as, for example, Japanese Sumo wrestling, and Bharata Yatnam dance of South India. But here is where they part company, for dance draws constantly upon the folk, popular and exotic reservoirs. Like all cultivated art forms, dance exists in a tense aesthetic environment in which the art is caught between a settling desire to fix itself in one perfect form, and an unsettling desire to "progress." And dance, like all the other art forms, has it both ways. The fixed "perfections" are relegated to museums or repertory, while the unsettling "progressions" vibrate throughout the market place. The audiences of these two extremes are in continual conflict, for those patrons and practitioners who are dedicated to progress tend to assume that the museum means death and the marketplace means life, while those who are given to conservation assume that the museum means art, and the market implies a dispensable commodity. There is truth to both sides, of course. A Merce Cun-

39

ningham experiment in dance has more vitality than does another Swan Lake by some European state ballet. But experiments in dance die fast and easy, and their litter is blown about into oblivion, not even to be given a decent burial. Only the best examples survive to be embalmed in a museum repertoire. Embalmed is not quite the right word, though, for the repertoire (or the art museum) is not a repository for artistic corpses, but for artistic be-ings whose capacity for self-resurrection makes for eternal life. The milestones remain: these are the museum-pieces which have the capacity for self-resurrection: but the developmental line is where the action is.

Popular athletic art forms do not share this characteristic of road and milestones. American football has gone through a century of permutations, but the rules, techniques and equipment of the days of The Four Horsemen do not go into repertory. Popular art forms do not have the capability for self-resurrection. They often become artifacts in an historical museum, as might Big Little Books, plaster statues of the Virgin Mary, or souvenir pennants, but they do not belong in a museum of the arts. Popular arts are far more receptive to reading humanistic meanings in, than to extracting meanings out. They are social documents that tell us about their audiences, while humanistic documents tell us that and much more, for within them we discover ourselves and we discover abstractions for which the works are emblematic, not as accidents of the moment, but as a design of artists.

This distinction between popular art and cultivated art can be useful. Popular works are not self-sustaining, because their meanings are thinly layered and tied to the moment. Great cultivated works have multitudinous layers of meanings in which all ages can recognize themselves. Popular works are destined for historical museums because they are products of their time and of their place; cultivated works are intended for art museums because they are products of human beings in their times and places. The eternal denominator is humanity, the shifting numerators are time and place.

This arithmetic image is worth pursuing, for it may serve to illuminate my method of comparing art forms. Let us imagine two art works side-by-side, and select one to place as eternal denominator and the other to place above it as numerator. Take, for example,

40

Myron's Discobolus and a photograph of John L. Sullivan au rampant.
Or the first game of the 1944 World Series and Martha Graham's 1944
Appalachian Spring. All four examples are "dated," that is, they
are clearly of a time and of a place, but they are not equally "dated."
There is a universality inherent to Discobolus and Appalachian
Spring that transcends 450 B.C. and 1944 A.D. and the Attic Pen-
insula and Manhattan Island. This inherent universality is clouded
over in the other two examples.

In addition to the characteristic of universality -- the eternal human
denominators --, cultivated art forms have another characteristic
that divides them from popular art forms, one which seems to be
opposed to universality. This is the characteristic of variety. There
is so much variety among the cultivated arts, that we cannot deal
with them en masse. We may speak of contemporary professional
wrestling as a collective noun; but we cannot speak of today's
dance or even ballet in such an inclusive manner. That is, while
it is possible for me to discuss the humanistic meanings of wrestling
without asking myself, "Which bout do I mean?," in dance, we
must ask, "Which kind of dance?" If the answer is ballet, then the
question follows, "Is it modern or romantic ballet?" If the answer
is romantic, the next question is, "Which ballet?" If the answer is
The Nutcracker, the next question is, "Which production?" If the
answer is New York City Ballet, the final question is, "Which performance?" In other words, dance, because of its variety and its
inherent capacity for change, does not lend itself easily to all-
inclusive generalities.

But to discuss things at the level of specific performances would convert this chapter into a critical review, and such is not my purpose.
Yet it is important to demark some aspect of dance for discussion,
some kind of dance which is an art form, designed for production
before an audience. Let us call that theatrical dance.

As I have said, the matter of audience is important, helping us to
distinguish professional wrestling from other athletic contests. In
like manner, audience distinguishes theatrical dance from other
dances. Selma Jeanne Cohen, in her "Prolegomenon to An Aesthetics of Dance," makes this distinction: "The [Indian] rain dance
succeeds when the rain falls. The square dance does well when the

performers have a good time. Only theatrical dancing is designed
to provide the observer with an aesthetic experience. In other
words, the rain dance is utilitarian and the square dance is a social
act. Both can be effective with or without an audience. But theatrical dance, whether it be classical ballet, ice follies, or underwater rockettes must have an audience, or it is only a rehearsal.
Athletic contests, on the other hand, can be "successful" without
an audience -- as many lonely college baseball coaches or high
school tennis coaches could attest. Only judges or umpires are
needed, but, (except for Olympic-style contests) the athletes are
not performing for the judges or any audiences. They are acting
toward a specific outcome, like rain dancers or medicine men, or
for recreation, like the square dancers. Finally, even Olympic
judges are not really an audience from whom an aesthetic response
is to be summoned up: a gold medal Olympic gymnast is not asked
to provide an experience for judge or audience. It is true that the
judgments that are made about Olympic performers are allied to art
and aesthetics, dealing with such abstractions as grace and poise
and beauty, yet the success of the gymnast does not depend on
consumer audience in search of an experience.

It may be, therefore, that art exists only where there is an audience,
just as sound exists only when there is an auditor. To speak of art
without speaking of response, communication, experience, feeling
or perception is almost meaningless, and all these terms presume an
audience. This definition of art brings up problems which need not
be discussed here (about anonymous and expressionist art, for instance), but it is useful at least to limit the field of art in both dance
and athletics.

There are very few European and American sports which are truly
theatrical, although there is nothing inherent in our athletics that
necessarily prevents an aesthetic or humanistic purpose. But it is
our western way -- most particularly our American way -- to quan-
tify rather than to humanize. For example, popular sports like
boxing, baseball and football have become statistical contests, with
elaborate systems of bookkeeping, and the disembodied voice of a
commentator operating both as a concurrent crutch for understanding
the statistical contest and as a buffer between the contest and the
audience, who often carry radios along with them to sporting events

42

presumably so that they will know how to respond. This kind of interpretive mediation is peculiar to modern popular culture experiences,
and its penchant for quantification further serves to separate the
spectators from a human experience, so far, in fact, that press agents
are hired to restore the attributes of humanity to the participants.
By contrast, people do not write of bull-fighting in terms of statistical records of weight of bulls, numbers of left-handed coups de
grace, weighing of round-robin tourneys, counting of votes for all-
star classics and counting of seconds for sudden-death playoffs.
Neither do prima ballerinas have photo-finish decisions on length
or height of leap, nor does the World Almanac publish world records
of number of pirouettes, or of record weights on lifts.

No, sad to say, in America, when athletics goes beyond win-or-lose
statistics, it apparently must don the mask of comedy. Professional
wrestling and the Harlem Globetrotters are the results. The Globetrotters are beyond competition -- they are potential artists -- but
their audience stops short at hilarity. Professional wrestling is primitive cathartic, but it is gross, extrovertive and phony. He who
leaves a Globetrotters contest or a professional wrestling match in
thoughtful silence may be ready for ballet; to the silent human American sports has reached its artistic limit. But there are some athletic
contests that go beyond statistical conflict.

Consider this. Bullfighting is honest, not phony. It really is a life
and death struggle, but what raises it to art is the fact that the matador puts death into the background, (where it is for you and me) and
he honestly devotes himself to that cliche of Quarterback Clubs and
American Legionnaires -- how the game is played. Similarly ballet
is art, not athletics. The dancer can do all that a gymnast does, but
athletic prowess is put into the same kind of background as that to
which death is relegated by the matador. The outcome matters little; what matters is how the "game" is played. Was the player
aware of his place in the Design? Did he contribute to the Design?
And ultimately what matters is this: did the artist communicate to
his audience -- individually, not as a mass -- an experience in
humanity and in design? At this point, I am being deliberately
equivocal in my use of the word design. I mean it partly as meaning
moral and cosmic design, as writers such as Ernest Hemingway have
found in bullfights a meaningful design in an irrational cosmos; but

43

I also mean the word to be understood in the technical sense of the visual arts, as the design in composition. The design of athletic contests is strategic design, not total artistic composition. No athlete takes his position on the field for reasons of artistic composition.

In dance, design is a total thing, occupying a space which becomes a totality because it is created into the design. This is true whether it be an Alvin Ailey pas seul or an extravagant finale to The Firebird. Indeed, this is one way of telling good dance from bad dance. Dance, as a physical thing, is "successful" insofar as it creates a totality of space. Dance is good when an audience can find no unused space in his view. By "unused space" of course I do not mean unoccupied areas, but space not taken into the design. This applies not only to dance, but to all the arts. And the ultimate success may be found in the extension of created space to the audience, once more individually, not en masse. The aesthetic experience of dance does not require zoom cameras, opera glasses, or front-row-center seats to focus experience, because it is a matter of space, not focus. In the final analysis, it is this straining of space, this reaching out to the audience that separates dance and bullfighting and wrestling from football, golf and track. The athletic arts are performed for the audience, the athletic sports are performed before the spectators.

Yet dance, bullfighting, and professional wrestling are very different from one another. The characteristics which differentiate them are content, design, and creativity. Wrestling is most limited in all of these -- it is a simplistic primitive experience with highly restrictive use of space, and caricatured protagonists. Bullfighting is conventionalized and ritualistic but it is genuine, and conscious of design, within a conventional setting. But as with wrestling and the athletic sports, the plot in the bull ring doesn't change. There will be shifts in power and advantage. There will be variations in technique, but the dualistic conflict remains the same. We versus they, good versus evil, man versus beast, life versus death. Yet in the bull-ring, there is the additional necessity to "do it beautifully." Aesthetics has a morality of its own that seems only to deplore accident and gracelessness. Accidents must remain inaudible and invisible. That is what went wrong with the Australian tag match in Madison Square Garden, where the accidental injury was

44

not incorporated into the total design. "Oops!" is not permissible in the athletic arts.

But it is creativity that most markedly differentiates dance from the other athletic arts, not only in the senses of originality and variety, and of the totality of created design, but in the abstract sense of the creation of space in time as an experience. Maxine Sheets, in The Phenomenology of Dance, says that "a dance as it is formed and performed, is experienced by the dancer as a perpetually moving form, a unity of succession, whose movements cannot be measured: its past has been created, its present is being created, its future awaits creation. Yet, it is not an externally related series of pasts, presents, future -- befores, nows, and afters; it is truly ekstatic, it is in flight, it is in the process of becoming the dance which it is, yet it is never the dance of any moment." These remarks are equally applicable to the audience as to the dancer, and thus, to answer the question of William Butler Yeats, you can't tell the dancer from the dance. ॰ . .

Which is all very fine-sounding, but how does this make it possible to distinguish dance from ice capades and water ballet, which are also "in flight?" To a certain extent, these popular art forms "cheat" on the medium -- the steel blades gliding on a virtually frictionless film of water on ice, the swimmers dancing in the denser medium of water serve to free the performers of the strictures of Newton's laws -- which is like bringing a microphone to the opera stage or a tranquilizer gun to the bull ring. Or providing toe shoes for the ballet artist.

This last physical aid may suggest how nebulous is the line between popular dance and cultivated dance. But the fact is that toe shoes are passé in most modern dance, and in most schools of dance, they are not introduced to the student until several years of barefoot practice have been completed. This is not the only example of a return to the elements in dance, because Jean Georges Noverre's reforms in the eighteenth century were of a similar nature. This suggests that the "cheating" media may mark a difference between cultivated dance and popular dance, for the media, it would appear, are a barrier to a humanistic experience. The Greek root for gymnastics -- gymnós, "naked" -- may bring our understanding of

athletic aesthetics into focus. With this in mind, it becomes apparent that the strictures, the conventions of the dance experience are
not determined by yardsticks and time clocks, but by the limitations
of man as man; bone and muscle in a medium of gravity and air.
What can humanity do within those limits -- and do it beautifully?
The question relates to very few other art forms, of course, since
most forms depend upon media to bridge the gap between artist and
audience -- musical instruments, paints and pencils, wood and stone,
films and projectors -- only theatre arts communicate directly with
the body, and only dance communicates without the potential barrier of language.

Returning to the arithmetic image of numerator and denominator, it
is clear that dance and non-verbal athletics always emphasize the
eternal human denominator, because their medium of expression is
the human body, which doesn't change. The closer the art is to
gymnós, the more likely it is capable of being universal. That is,
the presence of physical and verbal trappings can lead to the domi-
nance of the local numerator. In sports, for example, baseball and
football are boxed in by verbal restrictions and literary conventions
to the extent that the rules obscure the universals. An alien visitor
from another time would very likely find modern football to be about
as immediate an experience as an Ashanti would find a heavily
costumed eighteenth-century minuet. Similarly, the literary film
ballet of The Red Shoes probably would seem to be too overweighted
with conventions and external trappings to provide an immediate
human experience for a rodeo star.

However, this should not be understood as meaning that there is a
simple athletic aesthetic that nudity is best. What it means is that
art is best when the audience can discern the common denominator,
the universal humanity beneath the numerator of time and place.
Thus, an ice capades finale where skaters are propelled about enveloped in extravagant structures is no more humanistic an experience
than is a Rose Bowl float built on a GMC truck: the basic truth is
obscured. But Balinese dance, despite all its heavy ornaments and
involved designs, does not disguise the human being beneath, one
who is striving to carry herself with unified grace in a world of air
and gravity, of time and space.

46

One more disclaimer about over-simplified athletic aesthetics. Just as in an athletic contest the simple outcome of winning is not enough to the aficionado, so in dance, simply not making an error is not enough to the informed spectator. Few, if any, of my remarks about space, and time, and creativity, can be applied to performances which are technically weak. This is probably one of the main dividing lines between the appreciation of sports events and of the athletic arts. Both share a common aesthetic based upon concern with physical ability, strength, bodily control, stamina, precision and accuracy, but in the art form, this is all merely prerequisite to total aesthetic experience with design, meaning, and creativity. The ultimate experiences are rare, of course, and in anticipation of these moments, the spectator must bone up his technical sensibilities, to be able to tell good from bad in technical art, and, in athletic arts, to distinguish the excitement of a ninety yard touchdown run that results from a recovered fumble, (oops!) from the beauty of a perfectly designed and executed three-down march to the goal line.

This should suggest some conclusions that can be drawn from this discussion. One conclusion is that there is such a thing as athletic aesthetics which is an aspect of popular culture studies that merits serious examination, particularly where popular athletics have developed theatrical adjuncts such as ice shows, water ballet, professional wrestling, and exposition basketball. In the study of popular athletic theatre, dance is the cultivated art form that provides the most appropriate patterns for criticism, because dance is an art of bodily expression, in technique closer to athletics than theatre or symphonic music or the visual arts (although all of these are utilized in dance). On the other hand, toward answering the eternal conundrum, how does one tell what is "good" in art, the comparison of the cultivated form with related popular forms may be more profitable to the newcomer to the arts than would a regimen of exclusive high art theory and criticism. That is to say, a newcomer might do better to approach dance as athletics than to try to buy it as a complete culture-kit.

Is there anything "higher" or "better" about the cultivated athletic art form -- dance -- than there is about popular sports? I think the answer is undoubtedly yes, but I would insist that no one interpret this as implying my advocacy of an unvarying diet of dance for me or for anyone else, any more than the "higher" value of Hamlet,

Moby-Dick and Chateau La Tour du Pin Figeac should cause me to abstain from Ironside, Carry On Jeeves and Coca-Cola. Neither would I have it thought that all "ballet" is profound: much is merely extravagant entertainments and gymnastic show-pieces both in purpose and in execution. Ballet would be far less intimidating if it were not so invariably touted as an unrelieved punitive exercise in cultural elevation. Nevertheless, at its best, dance has a purpose that transcends technical prowess. Dance can be a form of communication of abstract ideals and mythic truths, and there is something higher in that which communicates than there is in that which is only a spectacle, or which exists only as an event to be computed into a record book. In dance, there is almost no limit to the variety of meanings about humanity and human relationships that can be expressed -- including rivalry, competition and combat -- which are the virtual extent of sports. The variety in dance is not restricted to content, however, for dance is varied in style, in progressive change and experiment, and in the resources that are drawn upon from the rich background of ethnic, folk, popular, recreational and ritualistic dance that exists.

If the general public were to understand the relationship between dance and athletics, one would think that the dance might be destined to grow in popularity. It should, for instance, be easy to move from skating as a sport, to ice shows, to ballet, and to retain an appreciation of each in its place; but, for the general public, the transfer might be difficult, because it is unfortunately true that many sports enthusiasts have no aesthetic appreciation of athletics to build upon. It is for their benefit that the crutches to perception are designed: the running commentaries, the civic rivalries, the insistence on quantified judgments, the zoom-lens visual aids, the instant replays and the skates are added. Thus, it is the popular audience and the popular medium of television that "ruined" professional boxing. For the popular audience, a kayo speaks louder than footwork, and the violence of a haymaker is easier on a spectator than the direct confrontation of finding himself mirrored in a work of art. And the direct confrontation requires the labor of learning the technical language, of seeing the total design in which the knockout punch is only one focal point.

But what is required most for the appreciation of the athletic arts is

for the spectator to pierce through the specifics of the numerator to discern beneath a human denominator wherein he can find humanity in the design. Once this is done, transference from one numerator to another is possible. Olympic figure skating is not that far from dancing Krishna, and <u>Discobolus</u> inheres to every athletic contest, even when our brother man is encased under layers of high-impact-plastic armor plate. But until the spectator has pierced the armor, he will be an aesthetic provincial, condemned to a wilderness of exotic arts and outlandish sports, where more cosmopolitan others are not lost or bewildered, but find universal man freshly in the human movements of the day, discerning the eternal in the times, and their own times as a part in the design of eternity.

The Wishbook as Popular Icon

Up to this point, the topics have been related to the performing arts and the interpretive arts. The remainder of this book will place emphasis on more concrete and more static art forms, such as the decorative arts and religious icons. Literature, of course, is on a borderline, for we can always deny the importance of the physical book as part of the literary experience. In one sense, it makes no difference whether or not one reads The Grapes of Wrath from a dog-eared crumbling paperback, or from the Limited Editions Club's two-volume edition, bound in rawhide and grass cloth, with original lithographs signed by Thomas Hart Benton. It is The Grapes of Wrath either way. And yet, the two descriptions I have given should exemplify the importance of the packaging of literature. Literature is a market commodity, and, since Gutenberg, in 1450 A.D., literature has undergone a series of popular revolutions fostered by technological industrial and marketing developments. Among the most recent of these has been the paperback revolution, which has in turn produced a trend toward illustrated book covers. Thus we find that the paperback and the expensive illustrated edition are equally much commodities, physical art objects, and media for imaginative and abstracted expression, capable of embodying social, psychological

and spiritual yearning. On the surface, these characteristics would seem to be separate. Certainly it is possible to separate the book as a commodity, from the book as art object, from the book as literature, from the book as cultural window. The mere existence of booksellers, bibliophiles, critics and social commentators as separate occupations will demonstrate that reality. But I would prefer to take on all the aspects in all their uneasy combinations. Rather than reducing the complexity of books by narrowing the scope of my study, I will reduce the complexity by taking popular literature at its simplest degree of literacy, in the elementary school primer, and at its most abundant form as commodity, in the mail-order catalog. In either primers or catalogs, however, the apparent simplicity of the examples should not mask the ravelled complexities of commodity, art object, literature and cultural window, or social mythology.

In wistful moments an archaeologist must dream of unearthing in Greece a Searsopolis Roebuckeles Katalog, or its equivalent in Egypt, Mexico, South Africa or Turkestan. At times the culture-diggers have come close to this dream, as in the tomb of Tutankhamen, but this is more akin to unearthing an encyclopedia of what a culture planned to be remembered by, than is it a candid catalog of everyday Egyptian life. Archaeologists have little to go on in studying earlier cultures, and it is remarkable how few artifacts it takes to keep them happy. A cuneiform table of royal accounts, a broken clay head from Tlitalco, an occipital ridge and a molar from Olduvai, rotted postholes from an Ohio moundbuilders' stockade; these representative fragments will yield notes in archaeological journals, a few Ph.D.s, and a slight broadening and deeping of our images of past civilizations.

Much more could be learned from disinterred mail-order catalogs, if the archaeologist's fanciful wish were granted. We would learn not only of the garments of men, women, and children, but of their undergarments as well; not only of the homes of the culture, but of the tools and materials which went to make those homes; not only of how things and people were measured and made, but of how they were maintained and repaired with the equivalents of glues and trusses, paints and tampons, auto tune-up manuals and Bibles, hydraulic jacks and vitamin pills. Even more: the archaeologist could tell us of the self-images and wishes of everyday men and women. He could gain for us a window on their worlds of realities and dreams.

51

In that respect the mail-order catalog is truly an American icon. In the most traditional sense, of course, the word icon is applied to the religious images of Byzantium. "To the Byzantines," the historian D. A. Miller tells us, "the icon was the physical memorandum of something beyond; the window (the term is often used) through which men may look into higher realms." The Byzantine icons with which most of us are familiar are mosaics, pieced together of glittering fragments. The personages depicted in them are conventionalized to the point of being quite indistinguishable from one another, and the rendering of perspective, size and color violate scientific realism in the quest for the higher reality of "something beyond." In addition, the icons were popular works of art for the Byzantine masses, not for the aristocrats, whose art was in the private world of illuminated books. But to the average Byzantine, all these apparent shortcomings were dissolved in the immediacy of the total impression.

The American catalog is remarkably similar, even to the irreverently reverent nicknames by which Americans express the mystical function of their icons: The Wish Book, The Big Book, The Farmers' Bible. Although each Big Book is a hefty unit, it is mosaic in structure, every item a glittering, if fragmentary, contribution to the totality. Even the "reverse perspective" of Byzantine art whereby psychological and spiritual importance dictate relative size and brilliance is reflected in the catalog-page layout. Thus, in the Montgomery Ward 1968 Christmas Catalog, the "Family Reference Bible" is larger than "young people's" or "study" Bibles. This technique, as well as the family emphasis, is as old as the catalogs, for the 1897 Sears Roebuck catalog shows the "Family Sunshine Range" and the "Home Sunshine Range" looming heavily over the spiritually diminutive "Othello" range and crass laundry stoves. Further, despite the fact that for nearly fifty years the catalog clothing has been photographed on living models, their faces and bodies are so nearly indistinguishable (including the recently added Afro-and Oriental-Americans) that it is difficult to recognize the same model in different costumes and poses. The models, like icon Christs, classical Greek statues, and Gibson's girls are conventional representations of the Ideal, not breathing individual beings. Readers of Vogue may identify with bony individualists, but catalog readers find the American Ideal in well-nourished equalitarians who transcend the ego. Not only are the models dissolved in mosaic anonymity, but the catalog writers

52

and photographers are as nameless as the artists of the old icons.

But to draw such technical parallels between traditional icons and mail-order catalogs is hardly more than a clever game. Is it fair and honest to extend these parallels to the totality? The Byzantine icon exists for a spiritual purpose. Is it valid to equate a material price-list with a spiritual symbol? To borrow from the argot of computer sales, the icon is a medium of software while the catalog is apparently no more than a material means to a hardware end. The icon unquestionably embodies the spiritual values of the culture. Does the catalog do this too? And if it does, what dismally material meaning does it give to our culture?

To get at answers to these questions, it is first necessary to recognize that the spirituality of an icon is not inherent to the object as such. That is, the object is an icon only to one who sees it as an image that means something to him. Hence, the Byzantine icon is not truly an icon to those of us who are not heirs to Byzantine Christianity. While the term is a convenient tag for discussing these objects as a class of artworks, they are not our icons. They are things to us, not meanings. Every culture, in this sense, has its own peculiar icons which will appear as mere things, not as meanings, to people of other cultures. The fact that the catalog is itself a material thing of things does not prevent its being an image of loftier meanings.

The mail-order catalog does have meanings to Americans. It is the Wish Book; it is the semi-annual installment on the American Dream. More: it is the semi-annual affirmation of the American Dream, because the catalog's Wishes and Dreams are thrown out every six months, like an accelerated version of primitive societies' annual death and rebirth of a god. It is the paradox of "the king is dead; long live the king." But few gods and kings have such ignominious and unceremonious ends as mail-order catalogs, which variously go out with the trash, kindle stove fires, are cut up for paperdolls, or drop, page by page, into rural privy pits. At the rare times that an old catalog is found or reprinted, it is regarded as an object of affectionate ridicule, not of reverence. There is not room in the American mind for yesterday's dreams any more than there is for yesterday's automobile. "Old deeds for old people," said that arch-enemy of materialism, Henry Thoreau, "new deeds for new;" and the

catalog echoes, "old things for old people, and new things for new." Thus, from the earliest of the catalogs to the present, there have been few pages given to old things. The 1897 Sears catalog has no period furniture; and although the 1969 catalog does -- even in 1908 the catalog carried "Roman" chairs --, it is because it is new to be old, particularly with such new transformations as: "COLONIAL BAR . . . Black vinyl spill rail and decorative panels padded with polyurethane" . . . "Grandma's 19th Century styling here with these 20th Century features * Large automatic over *Built-in rotisserie . . . Low as $279.95 cash electric. . . ."

Popular icons are sometimes discernable by the folklore which surrounds them, but, strangely, although there are catalog tales, they have been neither collected nor indexed. This is probably true because the mail-order catalogs are so intimately contemporary to most Americans' experiences. There must exist an infinity of catalog-in-the-outhouse jokes and fabliaux of elementary lessons in sex gleaned from the underclothing and pharmacy pages, but these tales apparently are too close to everyday American experience to warrant transmutation into fantasy and folklore. That is, the anecdotes which are current are simply factual recitations of individual occurrences which rather than being passed on as lore, serve only to evoke other factual anecdotes. For example, one mail-order customer's experience of a back-order delay is likely to be regarded as only slightly different from another customer's having been sent the wrong item. There is little raw material for fantasy and fiction at Wards and Sears, for, like a chess game, everything is above board. Horsetrading and traveling salesmanship, like politics and poker, are richly productive of folklore, because there is enough hidden underhand to permit the development of fiction. But the whole mail-order catalog experience is aboveboard, and the whole tradition is based on mutual trust. What few anecdotes there are about catalogs are stories which express some deviation from straightforward, aboveboard trust. Sometimes the deviation is on the part of the mail-order house, but since these errors are almost invariably rectified, they are not productive of any particularly lasting lore.

More often the deviation from aboveboard straightforward trust takes the form of trusting the catalog and the mail-order house beyond reason. Thus, when a Sunday-school teacher asks, "Where did Moses

get the Ten Commandments?" and the pupil replies, "From Sears Roebuck," the child's trust exceeds the aboveboard contract which the mail-order catalog is in reality. Adult consumers as well have been known to carry their trust to extremes. Shortly after the turn of the century, a customer dropped his Sears Roebuck watch on a sidewalk, and when it broke, he wrote to the company to complain. The request for a refund was shown to Richard Warren Sears who directed: "Write him that our watches are guaranteed not to fall on concrete sidewalks; and send him a new watch."

Trust is the essence of the mail-order catalog business, and that is one respect in which the catalog of material things is the icon of an abstract ideal, because there is an equalitarian dignity implied in such catholic reciprocity of trust between an institution and the masses. The credit for starting the tradition is due to Aaron Montgomery Ward, whose simple idea was to buy directly from manufacturers for cash and to sell directly to farmers, also for cash, and at a very low markup. His first "catalog" in 1872 was a single sheet. Two years later it had eight pages and bore the first true mail-order guarantee, that all items were sent by express "subject to examination." The most extreme version of the guaranteed trust was Richard Sears' "Send No Money" campaign, which began in 1900. Sears had entered the general mail-order business by way of watches which he sold retail at low enough prices that they could be resold by jewelers at a profit. By 1892, when Ward's catalog had expanded to over 500 pages and his gross income exceeded $1,000,000, Sears had given over half his catalog to goods other than watches and jewelry. Until 1900, goods were sold for cash, although Sears invited his customers to send their payments to his Minneapolis bankers, to be turned over to Sears only if they trusted him. Under the "Send No Money" agreement, orders were sent Collect On Delivery, but by 1902, with almost $800,000 worth of unclaimed and returned merchandise -- and catalogs in the hands of virtually the entire rural population of the United States --, Sears abandoned the practice, returning to the requirements that cash accompany the order. The "Send No Money" technique is still a valued means of winning trust and expanding markets, however, since in recent years the Spiegel firm, looking for a larger slice of the mail-order business, has employed a variation on Sears' old method.

The trust which Montgomery Ward and Richard Sears wanted to win from Americans was based on their knowledge of and respect for the shrewd and well-founded suspicion which farmers held for local merchants, who often operated without competition and took advantage of their monopolies. The catalogs strived to become entirely trustworthy. From the beginning, the pictures and descriptions of the items are enticing, but they are not exaggerated. Julius Rosenwald, who later succeeded Sears, and the first regular catalog editor, William Pettigrew, began the "healthy custom of calling skunk fur 'SKUNK' and dyed rabbit 'Dyed Rabbit,'" and of giving actual volume of kitchen utensils, and of guaranteeing horsepower of motors and engines. The verbal honesty is exemplary. In a 1937 review of the Sears catalog in The Saturday Review of Literature, Lovell Thompson wrote that "Sears offered free to American writers . . . a model of style . . . conscientious, frank, direct; it is hard to doubt the truth of what is said. . . . Sears knows the precise word when you don't."

Honest, aboveboard, precise wording is the essence of the catalogs' literary style. Very early, "copywriters were instructed to say 'sweat,' not 'perspiration;' 'go to bed,' not 'retire;' 'food,' not nutrition;' 'tears,' not 'lachrymal secretions;' and 'men and women' instead of 'ladies and gents.' Also taboo became phrases such as 'lowest prices in America,' 'world's largest dealer in lawn-mowers,' 'America's strongest work pants,' unless justified by actual fact." Precise wording in the modern catalogs includes unequivocal definitions of such terms as "sunfast," "preshrunk," "sanforized," "linear polyethylene," "BTU" and "automatic frequency control." Catalog terminology has even served to standardize the American language, as people in the provinces are obliged to order pictured items in the dialect of the Chicago-centered mail-order houses. What is still known in the rural South as a "sling-blade" or "slam-bang" must be ordered from a picture labelled "weed cutter." Apropos to standardizing, it is undoubtedly true that the acceptance by mail-order houses in 1941 of the age-size standards developed by the U. S. Bureau of Home Economics from WPA statistics was a major force in placing competing stores and manufacturers on an equal basis in stating sizes; just as the catalogs were the force which accustomed Americans to the one-price retail system rather than the old traditional marked-price-asking-price-selling-price system. In these and other ways,

the mail-order catalogs have become intimately woven into the very fabric of American life.

There are some snarled spots in the fabric, however. The values expressed by this icon are not all positive. On the retail level, the catalogs reflect the perennial American quarrel between nationalism and regionalism. The nationalizing threat of the catalogs was fought by local merchants who saw the catalogs as instruments to draw money out of town, although they themselves bought their goods from out of town wholesalers. Consequently, loyal rural and small town consumers bought from the catalogs with a feeling of guilt. In 1903, Richard W. Sears promised to ease the guilt by refraining from placing his firm's name on any "box, package, wrapper, tag, envelope or article of merchandise." The merchants countered by spreading rumors of cheap quality goods, by telling jokes about one-dollar mail-order sewing machines that turned out on arrival to be a needle and a spool of thread, and, in the South, by promoting whisper campaigns rumoring that Richard Warren Sears was a Negro. Another snarl in the fabric which disturbs the big mail-order houses today is the "hick" stigma which remains from pre-war years, when catalogs were almost exclusively directed toward rural needs. In the depression year of 1937, the Sears Spring and Summer catalog cover exemplified the sales target of their catalog by depicting a wholesome young couple on a hilltop overlooking their John Steuart Curry farm. Reviewing this catalog as "Eden in Easy Payments," Lovell Thompson regarded it as a "guide to rural America" with "New York . . . the serpent in Sears' garden." Today, however, all the major catalogs direct their sales campaigns toward the urban serpents; yet the hick-stigma is still discernable both in the tone of bravado and in the rational apologies (footnoted from that icon of sciencism, Consumer Reports) which are employed by urbanites who have bought goods from one of the catalogs or one of their modern retail outlets. These retail stores, incidentally, are not to be regarded as icons, for, like the J. C. Penney stores and A&P Supermarkets, the retail stores are too public, too tied to personalities and local associations to be icons. The catalog, on the other hand, is a household window looking out upon things beyond the local horizon.

The pre-World War II catalog did indeed represent a bucolic Garden of Eden; but the urban-directed post-war catalogs, the expansion of

57

the chains of retail stores, and ultimately, the addition of such
sophisticated new lines as "designer" clothes and original art works
in the 1960s marked a social reversal. To retain the Edenic image,
the Garden of Eden invaded the very atelier of the serpent, New
York City. The Garden remained strangely innocent, for art, clothing and furniture in the catalog never became confused with class-
consciousness. The catalogs remained books of things, and the things
remained achievable, all clearly marked with an unambivalent price-
tag, all clearly designated as Good, Better or Best in material quality. Even in the serpentine metropolis, every man enters the catalog's Eden on equal footing. Things may have different prices, but
one man's dollar is as good as another's. Such classless ideals do
not enhance snobbery.

In assuaging the guilt about hick-stigma, Sears Roebuck has been most
resourceful in fighting fire with fire, or converting the out-of-date to
the nostalgic; but, in addition to wiring "Grandma's stove," selling
reproductions of 1897 catalog pocket-watches, and (in 1968) baldly
labelling their Christmas catalog a "Wish Book" -- including in it
such urbanely wished-for items as a $1600 suit of Toledo armor and a
$3300 diamond pendant --, Sears has engaged as "consultants" Sir
Edmund Hillary and Vincent Price. The Vincent Price art collection
was not Sears' first foray into the art field, nor was it a sudden leap
into high-quality aesthetics. In 1944, a year in which more than two
hundred items were listed as unavailable due to war shortages, Sears
offered canvas-finish oil-painting reproductions of famous American
paintings, including George Inness' Peace and Plenty which also
served as the cover illustration. The Sears Fall and Winter catalog
in 1969 offered only five art reproductions (at $5.99 and $9.99,
exquisitely framed), but one can hardly go wrong aesthetically with
well-selected works by Rembrandt, Fragonard, Cezanne, Van Gogh
and Picasso. Similarly, when the Vincent Price mail-order collection of original prints was introduced in 1963, no one could question
the quality of the selections. Nonetheless, Frank Getlein, writing
in the New Republic, seemed to feel that some cheapening of fine
art had occurred. This may not have been his intended meaning,
for his prose, unlike that of the catalogs, has a serpentine ambiguity
and scaly irony. Sears "pays art the supreme mercantile compliment
of treating it as merchandise," he wrote. "The art of Sears seems
to come under the homefurnishings department, as it does for the vast

majority of Americans who ever buy a print or painting . . . ."

Which brings us back to the mail-order catalog's office as popular
icon. An icon should be a "window through which men may look
into higher realms" at the same time that it embodies essential values
of its culture. The surface values of American culture expressed in
the Wish Book are values of material well being, of middleclass
equality and of democratic mutual respect. There is another, pro-
founder, value which grows out of these others. Alexis de Tocque-
ville identified it and named it "indefinite perfectibility." This is
the higher realm on which the catalog provides a window. The material things are there, and they are achievable. All things achievable bear a price-tag, even works of art, and all can be labelled
Good or Better or Best, despite the fact that today's Best may be
demoted to tomorrow's Better. Such is the way of indefinite perfectibility. In six months there will be a new window on even higher
realms of material well-being. And that well-being will be attainable, too. Even as early in catalog history as 1917, Scribner's magazine extolled the moral honesty of the catalog's "quiet, steadying
mission" to be concerned "frankly with mere things." Within these
limits, the catalog "does not set us longing for more than we can
possibly buy," nor does it make a claim to purveying the things that
money cannot buy. The catalog sells Bibles, not salvation. The
catalog sells Best quality trousers, not best quality taste. The catalog sells genuine art works, not genuine taste.

The New Republic' comments on the mail-order sales of original
Rembrandts, Callots, Whistlers and Calders suggest a conflict in values. If art is not merchandise; if art is not homefurnishings, then
what is it? If art is not for home and family, if it is not things like
the Family Sunshine Range or the Family Reference Bible, what transcendent no-thing can art be? Is art only for kings and aristocrats?
But the American Dream is the one that Huey Long reduced to a slo-
gan: every man a king. Hence, if art is for kings, art is presumably
for every American. Or, is art to be revered and viewed only on
sabbath afternoons in secular temples? To do so, is to revere things,
not ideals, and the catalog-icon resists the whole idea of reverence
for material things. Artworks, stoves, Bibles and mail-order catalogs
are themselves things, material transitory and replaceable. Thus, it
is a paradoxical possibility that the catalogs of things, resting on a

tradition of mutual trust, help American consumers to distinguish between material things that money can buy and higher values that money cannot. The trust, once destroyed, could not be replaced; the catalog can be replaced. Ward's, Sears, Spiegel's, Penney's and Alden's deliver the goods, but should they cease to deliver the goods, reverence will not prevent iconoclasm. Old icons for old men; new icons for new.

The mail-order catalog, then, is an American popular icon for more reasons than its mosaic structure. Intertwined in the fabric of daily life, it influences basic behavior patterns of domestic economy and of language, and most of all it fulfills the quasi-religious function of providing an affirmation of the attainment of the dream of those who emigrated to America; a dream of sharing equally in the material produce of the society. Patterns of deeper meanings, infinitely complex, are discernable as well. The icon is classless, yet distinguishes between the old, which is obsolete and outcaste, and the new, which must be kept new in semi-annual reincarnations. Unlike most ritual reaffirmations, this icon is different in every rebirth. The unfathomable paradox of the American mind is that the unchanging value is change itself. The carrot moves before the donkey, the fruit eternally eludes Tantalus, and the mail-order catalog draws Americans forward with wishes of something better. But the wish-function of the catalog passeth all understanding, for its wishes are attainable. It is true, of course, that all Americans cannot buy all they wish for, just as it is regretably true that all Americans do not share equally in the nation's well-being. The catalog rests on an assumed general equality, and the assumption is not ill-founded, for some of its goods will be found in homes on Indian reservations, in Appalachian cabins and in urban slums. For the Americans in these places, the icon function of the Wish Book is intensified, not denied. Finally, and compounding all the other paradoxes, is the apparent fact that the uncompromising materialism of the icon and its mosaic bits reassure consumers of eternal spiritual values; that is, there are things that money cannot buy. Those things, the icon means, cannot be reissued in newer, better forms every six months.

Returning at last to the possibility of mail-order catalogs for past civilizations, it is clear that the speculation is fanciful because the mail-order catalog is at once image and product of the uniquely

American experience. This is true not only for this popular icon, but it is true in the higher arts, where "cataloging" is a style of nationalistic expression that has been employed by such artists as Walt Whitman, Hart Crane and Charles Ives to evoke the sweep and conflicting variousness of the unity which is America. Even more, the speculation is fanciful because the very concept of the Wish Book is posited on the achievement of one of the great wishes of mankind, the wish for universal literacy. Without universal literacy there could be no book of material wishes for the masses of men and women. The Wish Book of things is reserved for those fortunate people whose three magic wishes have already been granted: democracy, literacy and reciprocal trust.

The Genesis of Dick and Jane

Dick and Jane, of course, are the names of the hero and the heroine
of the leading primary reading textbooks of the United States. If you
were between the ages of six and forty-five in 1970 the odds are better than fifty-fifty that Dick and Jane provided you with your first
direct literary experience. If Dick and Jane didn't teach you to
read, the chances are close to one hundred per cent that you learned
with an analogous brother and sister and family from some textbook
published by a firm other than Dick and Jane's Scott, Foresman and
Company. You may remember such wholesome residents of Textbook
Town as Alice and Jerry, Joe and Jane, Tom and Jane, Ben and
Alice, Tom and Betty, or Ted and Sally. If you are very young, you
may have learned with Scott, Foresman's black children, Penny and
Mike. If you are English, you may have learned to read with Betty
and Tom, if you are Filipino, it could be that you will remember
Pepe and Pilar. In some nations, you may have learned with a
translation of Scott, Foresman's Dick and Jane.

By sheer weight of numbers, therefore, the primer is a matter of
popular culture. By token of being composed of stories with illustrations, the primer can be regarded as an art form, although it is far

more likely to be regarded as a purely utilitarian school book. The aesthetics of the primer reflect the times, and so are best examined by studying the primer's historical development against the backdrop of social and political change in America.

The success story of the Dick and Jane books begins about 1930, but the story of the art form that dominated primary education starts in rudimentary forms at the beginning of the century. A more useful starting point, however, is with Cora Wilson Stewart, whose administrative and honorific titles sound like straight-lines from Grand Old Opry: she was the Founder of the Moonlight Schools and the President of the Kentucky Illiteracy Commission. Mrs. Stewart, in 1915, wrote a reading primer for unlettered adults of the rural hill country of Kentucky, adults who she said, "somehow missed their opportunity" to learn to read when they were children, and who, unlike the foreigners who flooded into American cities in the decades before the First World War, had no opportunity for evening instruction in electrified modern city schools. Mrs. Stewart's answer to rural illiteracy was evening instruction on "moonlight evenings" when farmers and 'croppers and their wives might find their ways along the ruts and bends to the one-room school houses where many of their children had unwillingly spent the sunlit days, itching and wiggling through monosyllabic short-short fantasies of "I see the hen," "The rat is in the hat," or "The dog and the cat chat." Thus, Mrs. Stewart's honorific titles are compassionate, missionary and dignified, and her book, the First Book of the Country Life Readers, is an ideal starting point for an examination of primers and textbooks as popular art objects.

Her primer represents the archetypal characteristics of all American primers more directly than we can ordinarily discern them in the books designed for little children. The ennobling mission of our American educational system shows more clearly; yet, the potentials for possible misuse and abuse stand out especially clearly, too, for the moonlight primer is an inculcator of established norms, a propaganda tool for the American good life of progress, education, family, Bible and plumbing. Today, and for a quarter of a century now, it has been fashionable to question these middle-class values, to challenge the institutions that perpetuate them, and to ridicule and oust such insidious, incompetent and bigoted primary tools of the

63

establishment as the lowly novels of Dick and Jane, popular heroes of mid-America. Of Dick and Jane, of their detractors, their imitators, their births and their deaths, more later, but let us first look more closely at the 1915 primer for adults.

In order to do this properly, it will be necessary to read the section in small print at the beginning, the "Suggestions to Teachers" that most of us, as children, believed to be some arcane secrets that gave the teacher her power over us. Mrs. Stewart's "Suggestions to Teachers" are in reality like most others. She points out the logical structure of her primer, and she insists upon the relevant application of her lessons: they are not to promote reading as an abstract art, but to show that reading is a useful tool, useful for profit, for pleasure, for health, for community and for spiritual improvement. She knows her audience well: poor but proud Protestants who are unfortunately subject to chicanery and manipulation by a dominant society of literates. So, with Baptist directness, she wastes no time on ritual sprinklings and later confirmation but immerses them fully into membership in the American mainstream. On the seventeenth page, for example, she presents a lesson in checkwriting, and her "Suggestions to Teachers" state that "a supply of blank checks should be provided in advance." The rationale for a checking account has previously been established.

> I keep my hens in the coop.
> I keep my horses in the barn.
> I keep my pigs in the pen.
> I keep all my things in place.
> A bank is the place to keep money.
> I will keep my money in the bank.

The argument is realistic, and so are the checks. The realities of full citizenship are similarly presented. On a later page the moonlight student learns how to vote. Teachers are advised to provide ballots for a mock election, but there is no mockery of the process of election. "After the voting is over, the ballots that are imperfect should be destroyed; a careful count should then be made of the remaining ballots . . ." Following this the lesson preaches:

> With his vote a man rules.

64

The man who does not vote has no voice in the affairs
of his country.
He cheats his country, his family, and himself.
. . . .
The man who sells his vote sells his honor.

A man may rule with his vote, but women could neither vote nor
rule in 1915. They could, however, go to the moonlight school, and
could derive direct benefits from reading. In one illustration, a
prim, sunbonneted young woman in a fresh apron is shown standing
in the sunbathed entrance to a kitchen where an unkempt, bent-
over woman, surrounded by pots and pans and a picture hanging
askew on the wall, engages her in a dialogue:

"How fresh and sweet you look!
"I have just had my bath. I take a bath every day."
"Why do you do that?"

And so on, with explanations about clear skin, clean pores and a
classification of kinds of baths possible to hill people: sponge,
shower with a bucket, and tub or stream. Cleanliness in food prep-
aration is next:

Here you are, Mr. Fly.
I know where you have been.
. . . .
You have been to the slops from the sick man.
You have been feeding on a dead dog.
. . . .
I know what you will do with this filth.
You will drop it into my soup.
You will put it in the baby's milk.

. . . .
I will kill you, Mr. Fly.

Mrs. Stewart's frontal attacks on ignorance may be brief but their
scope is broad: the purity of the night air is asserted, as are the
evils of the boll weevil; and the virtues of rotating crops, of deep
plowing, of planting eroding stream banks, of spraying fruit trees,
of sheltering wagons from the elements, and of feeding ensilage to

cattle are all demonstrated by comparison of good farms with bad
farms. Several pages are given over to urging wives to vary their
cooking with limited foods: seven ways to cook potatoes, six kinds
of corn bread ("pone, hoecake, muffin, butter cake, corn dodger
and spoon bread"), and an all-corn dinner with six different ways of
preparing corn! ("Thank you for your plan. I will cook corn many
ways, but I do not care to eat a corn dinner"). Mrs. Stewart knows
her audience. Their presence at school indicated willingness to
change, but they are not to be hoodwinked by silly menus such as
the all-corn dinner, or foods they cannot afford. They know about
leavened yeast bread, but they cannot afford yeast cakes, so Mrs.
Stewart includes a two-page dialogue about how to grow your own
starter from one yeast cake, so that your husband can have "light
bread" every week, for:

> God made man.
> Woman makes bread.
> It takes the bread
> That woman makes,
> To sustain the man
> That God made.
> But the bread
> That some women make,
> Would not sustain any man
> That God ever made.

Yet man cannot live by bread alone; he needs meat as well, but not
fried three times a day . . . "you can roast, broil, or bake it; you
can also boil it or stew it." Then, too, there is food for the spirit:
"The wild flowers are in bloom. I enjoy them when I walk in the
fields and woods; don't you?"

"No, I do not. I scarcely see them when I go walking . . . I
scarcely know one from another. I only know that one flower is red
and another blue."

"Then you have missed half the joy of country life." The "Suggestions for Teachers" calls for the students "to bring in as many vari-
eties as possible of wild flowers," to be named by students, teacher,
and a reference book together. Yet aesthetic sustenance is not the

end of the course; that is reserved for several rural parables of Jesus, Moses' word to the children of Isreal of "A land wherein thou shalt eat bread without scarceness . . . When thou hast eaten and art full, then thou shalt bless the Lord thy God for the good land which he hath given thee," and thence to Ralph Waldo Emerson's simple thanksgiving, "Father in heaven, we thank Thee."

The Country Life primer, like nearly all primers, is a microcosm of American values, but only the Country Life primer has a fly venting its filth in the great melting pot of prosperity. In this sense, the Country Life primer is transitional in the history of American primers; indeed, the negative images and anecdotes would be anachronistic were this a child's primer of 1915, but for the moonlight students, a primer-America like Moses' land "without scarceness" would be a lie too easily disproven. The Country Life primer, therefore, employs negative realism as a literary device to win a worldly-wise and skeptical audience at the same time that it is used for propaganda purposes, to promote sanitary habits. Earlier primers used more abstract negative techniques, from the colonial New-England Primer's "In Adam's fall we sinned all" through The Tract Primer's nineteenth-century "I, is for Isaac, like Jesus he lies, Stretched out on the wood, a meek sacrifice." The Country Life moonlight primer is transitional in another respect. Prior to 1915, religious Christian values might be expected to be part of a primary reader, but 1915 marks the latest date in schoolbook publishing that it would be likely to find overtly religious-moral selections (such as Jesus' parable of the sower) included in a public school book, especially when it is combined with a direct purpose of learning to read the Bible, as Mrs. Stewart makes explicit as one of the goals of her reader in the third lesson. Undeniably there are moral and ethical parables in later readers - "later" both in publication and in grade-level - but most of these express secular and social values, and they are more likely to be oblique than direct in approach, stated without the epigrammatic morals of some of the selections in McGuffey's Readers. Cora Wilson Stewart was writing for the Bible Belt and her religious selections were appropriate to that principally Protestant audience.

But religious propaganda stands out openly in this primer; there is nothing insidious about its presentation. Religion, however, is not the real reason for this primer's existence nor for the combat of

illiteracy, as had been the case from the time of the 1647 "Old Deluder" common school law of old New England well on into the nineteenth century. Neither is literacy for good citizenship in a representative democracy the predominate rationale behind this reader as it had been in McGuffey's Readers that came into being in the 1840s, surviving even into the mid-twentieth century era of Dick and Jane. As the examples above have shown, both religious attitudes and literate citizenship are goals of the Country Life reader, and a sort of transcendental aesthetic as well; yet economic and social betterment -- material well being and popular acceptance -- are more apparent. The kingdom of heaven is a worthy goal, and the informed exercise of one's political franchise is a precious responsibility, but clean pores, clean teeth, a "garage" for the farm wagon, and a neat house, painted in an acceptable suburban hue are essential to full participation in American life. The 1915 Country Life reader is indeed a transitional primer.

Its value goals are particularly apparent because of its unique audience: regional, rural, poor and adult. But only a dozen years later another primer, this designed for children, was written for a select minority audience of Roman Catholics, and its overt religious training does not obscure the equally important purpose of secular training for membership in the American middle-class. This is the primer of The Rosary Readers, written by Sister Mary Henry of the Dominican Order of Sinsinawa, Wisconsin and published by Ginn and Company in 1927. Sister Henry's book appeared in the same year as did an anonymous child who was to become "Dick." His modest debut was in a small book that Scott, Foresman and Company of Chicago had developed for use in midwestern one-room schools, but in reality, the Rosary primer foreshadowed every detail of the next three or four decades. It is easy to see why the Rosary primer didn't achieve fame, however, as it is full of such embarrassing "unAmericanisms" as genuflexions, divine intervention and icon-covered altars. A close look at the secular details, however, will establish the pattern for other primers.

First, it is episodic in form, sort of like James Joyce's Dubliners, a novel of short stories which are connected by a single urban environment and a cadre of continuing characters, in this case a family of four: Peter, Jane, Father and Mother (plus a bonus of the Other Mother: "Oh! Oh! Oh! Now I know! Mary, Our Blessed Mother,

is everybody's mother."); the storekeeper, a foundling black puppy named Sport, a gift kitten named Mew-Mew, and in one episode, a nameless "big black dog."

The stories are realistic. There is no fantasy or fairy tale. The situation, while set in an environment of security and upper middle-class prosperity, are within the possible experience of most children: getting up in the morning, eating breakfast, going to the store, finding a puppy, little sister getting lost and being found, and so on.

The illustrations are naturalistic, but in the mode of the day in both style and content. Peter and Jane's home is Dutch colonial, with sunporch, fireplace, white tiled bath, lavatory on a single pedestal, dining room with a dark wood buffet. The family tends to dress up rather than down, and in good 1927 style. The clean pen-drawn illustrations relate directly to the story, although none tell the story. Their graceful curves, simple outlines, and convoluted treatment of hair, are reminiscent of art nouveau, but there is no use of line for decoration, abstract or otherwise. Beyond the delicate ruddiness of the cheeks, the pastel color is not applied with "painterly" technique, but merely fills in pen-outlined areas in flat, but transparent, reddish browns and blue-greens. The children and their mother have lovely profiles with the gently concave noses and slightly protruding upper lips that came into vogue with the Pre-Raphaelite and reached mass popularity with the academic styles of the later nineteenth century. There are 73 of these illustrations on the 122 pages, larger and more frequent at the beginning than at the end. It is, in short, an attractive book for 1927, with a style and color of illustrations similar to the fashionable advertisements that would appear in <u>Good Housekeeping</u> or <u>Scribner's.</u>

These are the literary and artistic characteristics of most primers of the period 1930-1970: episodic novels in form, realistic and middle-class in literary style, naturalistic and modish in picture style. These terms may seem rather elevated and sophisticated to apply to elementary school textbooks, but I employ them deliberately to emphasize that these books are not merely technical manuals and sourcebooks for printed words, but a form of popular art.

Dick and Jane, therefore, are not heroes born like Adam and Eve,

without ancestry; but neither are Sister Henry's Peter and Jane. At least two primers published a year earlier, in 1926, make use of continuing main characters in real-life situations. Scribner's Good Reading primer, for example, tells the teacher that "By keeping the same characters throughout the book, a story thread connects all the lessons. The use of the well known and much loved folk tales as a basis has been consciously avoided. . . . Although their value as reading matter is unquestioned, children have many other interests which these stories alone do not satisfy. . . ." So the authors say, but their continuing characters possess no distinction as characters; their names, Sam and Nell, do not appear until page fourteen, and then their teacher, Miss Gray, upstages the children and slips in some "well known and much loved folk tales," viz., "Jack be nimble." Furthermore, the restricted family, the strongly individualized characters, and the uncluttered contemporaneousness of Peter and Jane, Dick and Jane and all their imitators are absent in Good Reading. In a word, it lacks literary unity. The illustrations are strong, with heavy outlines like leaded glass windows. They are Tiffany without the jewel tones of art glass.

In the same year, 1926, The Lincoln Reader primer was an attempt to combine continuing real-life characters with folk tales. The motives of the authors are reasonable, but the results are somewhat monstrous. The "Introduction" states that "Reading material which emphasizes the familiar, the here and now, makes a strong appeal to children because they are interested in the familiar experiences of childhood. . . ." But also in this primer the stories are sometimes "very like the old folk tale in its rhythmic and repetitive form, because the familiar nursery tales and jingles have a sure appeal for children." The realism is again in the typical family, mother, father, Billy Boy, Betty Girl, baby sister, and several pets, but the authors' impatience to be "classical" in the manner of the story of the gingerbread boy produces:

> Billy Boy met Big Pig.
> "Gr-r! Gr-r! Gr-r! I can run, too. . . ."
> "Big Pig, I am going to school.
> I ran away from Brown Puppy.
> I ran away from Big Dog.
> I can run away from you, too."

70

This, we are to believe, is a typical morning walk to school, here and now.

Continuing back among the precursors of Dick and Jane, in 1924 The Laidlaw Readers Primer had been considerably more successful in achieving consistent real-life continuing characters at the same time that the old standard tales were included. The family of five lives in a richly appointed brick urban home, with window seats in every room, a library, and a charming garden. The children are vaguely "the boy" and "the girl" until page twenty-two where they become Tom and Ann. They do not have such harrowing adventures as Billy Boy and Betty Girl had, but they do drive out to Grandfather's farm in their new car. Tom is immediately impressed with grandfather's brick chimney. "Yes," grandfather says, "we have a brick chimney. The house is not brick. It is made of wood. What a big car you have, Tom. Can Father go fast?" Two pages after, grandfather continues, "We have an old house. It is not made of bricks. It is made of wood, you see. The brick chimney is old, too." Later in the primer, Tom is back at grandfather's house and, possibly a bit fearful that grandfather will start in on the chimney again, he brings a book along, from which grandfather reads "The Billy Goats Gruff and the Troll" and "The Three Pigs" (wherein the words brick and chinmey can once more be put to good use). The illustrations in this primer are similar to the Rosary Reader in style and in upper middle class content, but they are more detailed.

But before getting to the ultimate genesis of Dick and Jane, it would only be just to comment on the repetition of brick and chimney in the primer, for it is customary for adults to make fun of elementary readers -- especially primers -- because of their repetitive "Run, Dick, run" sentences. It should be borne in mind that formal and technical research into the teaching of reading has quite properly been directed toward words and language, from the abecedarians (A, B, C's) through phonics to modern linguistics. Community interest in teaching of reading has ordinarily been misinformed about such technical aspects of reading; indeed, almost no one other than primary grade teachers, professors of education and editors of reading books really understand whatever is the current theory of reading. This has not, of course, prevented community criticism of reading instruction, but this criticism usually relates to social development, and to the use of reading

to perpetuate values of the community. The technical aspects of reading may be superficially attacked, but ordinarily the real object of attack is the value system.

Either approach, the professionals' or the community's, regards the narrative and the illustrations merely as vehicles for the more important goals of learning to read or learning community values. It is these vehicles for primary training that are the subject here, because they are truly a popular art, belonging to competitive book publishers, all vying for an audience of six-year-olds with no interest either in how their reading ability is facilitated or in how their psyches are being manipulated into the community patterns of the establishment. They are interested in being interested. The primer that wins the child's interest at the same time that it effectively teaches reading skills and reinforces community values is the primer that gains popularity, and consequently, profit. But the children, for a variety of reasons, cannot select their favorites quite so freely as eight or ten years later they will select their hit records or film stars. Consequently, teachers try to surmise what will hold their pupils' attention, while publishers try to anticipate what will engage the interest of the teacher. At the theoretical level, this has polarized opinions of nature of the child's mind for more nearly a century and a half in America.

At one pole is the view that the child is absorbed in a world of reality and can be most easily interested by the familiar. This can be generally traced back to the late-eighteenth-century Swiss educator, Pestalozzi, and from him through his student, the German Froebel, who originated kindergartens, to Horace Mann, of Massachusetts, and another Yankee, Colonel Francis Wayland Parker, who brought Froebel's theories to the Midwest at the dawn of this century. Probably the simplest explanation of this realistic view is Horace Mann's account of Pestalozzi's "revelation." The Swiss had "first used engravings of objects; then, when a child said, but there's a ladder outside, 'The boy is right,' said he, 'the reality is better than the counterfeit; put away the engravings, and let the class be instructed in real objects.'" The "moonlight" Country Life adult primer follows this philosophy as we have seen in the use of blank checks, election ballots and woodland wild flowers. The reading symbols, in other words, are references to a material world which we call

reality, and the school will be most effective if it relates the symbols
to their real referents.

This is convincing, and one might wonder what arguments could come
from the opposite pole of unreality, or fantasy. Up until recent
years, actually, the only argument has been popularity, as implied
in the Lincoln Readers' primer in reference to the "nursery tales and
jingles" with their "sure appeal." Today, with a half-century of
Freud and Jung behind us, many of us are convinced that human
beings are by nature myth-making animals and that the fantasies of
our subconscious and unconscious minds are another kind of reality,
universal and inescapable. In projective psychoanalytical testing,
for example, it has been found by some investigators that children
more readily project themselves into pictures of "animals" in social
situations than into pictures of people; hence, the Children's [The-
matic] Apperception Test (CAT).

Such is the theoretical ground upon which Dick and Jane are pitted
against the billy goats, the three pigs and the little red hen. The
conflict is epic and the field sometimes wavers, sometimes swings
toward reality, sometimes toward fantasy. These are the swings of
"the educational pendulum," a cliche that is familiar to any serious
American school teacher of mature years. That the pendulum really
operated is unquestionable. Folk tale fantasy dominated from 1910
to 1930; Dick and Jane realism was dominant from 1931 to 1971, and
in 1971, it succumbed once again to fantasy, at least to a degree.
The reasons for the swing of the pendulum are complex, but it might
be said that the decade of the sixties showed the community, the
teachers and the publishers, that "reality" is too ambiguous and too
complicated and too painful to express in the representational simplicity of the mid-century primer. Pain, ambiguity and complicated
interrelationships of humanity, nature and institutions, however, are
the business of myth, where the irrational is represented in other-
worldly forms. It is doubtful, of course, that this kind of thinking
is what causes the publishers to change. They are business people,
and they are responding to market pressures on their branch of popular culture; yet, in the midst of all the swings of taste, popularity
and values, there is still the business of teaching reading, where
again pendulums swing between silent reading for meaning, and
reading as an echo of oral communication. Therefore, let us not

be overly hasty to laugh at grandfather's garrulity about his wooden
house with a brick chimney: the abstract symbols which we "read"
as brick and chimney will be a link between the material truth of
the American child's house, and the mythic exemplum of foresight
and industry which we know as the "The Three Little Pigs and the
Big Bad Wolf."

The literary technique of the Lincoln Readers primer is the "play
within a play," or the " set piece" contained within a novel, such
as we might observe in Dickens' Pickwick Papers, Huxley's Crome
Yellow and Warren's All the King's Men, where we either hear some-
one tell a tale, or we look over the shoulder of a writer. A variant
of this technique is used in the penultimate ancestor of Dick and
Jane, The Kendall Primer of Calvin Kendall and Caroline Townsend
(1917). The authors say that their primer "introduces children to the
printed page by means of a delightful continued story. It depicts the
adventures of Bob and Betty, with Rab their dog and Tab their cat,
their father, mother and baby sister, and their friends John and
Jean. . . . They live the normal lives of happy little American
children." In illustrations, once again, we see a prosperous family,
clad in the mode of the day, gathered together, mother sewing in
her mission-oak chair. In a garden view we see a New England
landscape, a fieldstone fence behind the children, low mountains
beyond that. The children are playing, Betty and Jean on the swing,
"John and Bob like to swing the girls." Following this is Robert Louis
Stevenson's "The Swing." Similarly, when the boys go to help father
make hay, two related rhymes follow, "Willie boy, Willie boy, where
are you going?" and "Little Boy Blue." Again, when the children
play school, a traditional ABC mnemonic follows, though no longer
is A for Adam, whose sins are ours, but "A is for Apple, so round and
red."

A significant difference between The Kendall Primer and the Lincoln
primer points up the difference between 1917 and 1926: in The Kendall Primer the children ride to the city; in the Lincoln primer, they
ride to the country to grandfather's farm. Like most of the Kendall
Primer, this travel story is written as a play dialogue between Bob
and Betty (for pupils to read in parts), a literary device that is also
used in what appears to be the earliest American primer to include
a typical family as continuing characters. This is Bobbs-Merrill's

<u>Child</u> <u>Classics</u> primer, by Georgia Alexander, first published at
Indianapolis in 1909, but still in print eleven years later. Herein
the picture style is much closer to that of Walter Crane and other
heirs of William Morris than in any of the later primers. The environment is wholly rural and delightfully prosperous. The boys have
a goat cart, their dog is a St. Bernard named Carlo, they eat their
own farm turkey at Thanksgiving. Curiously, father wears a three-
piece suit and it appears that he is a Yale man, since Frank wears
a "Y" sweater. The "Suggestions to Teachers" starts with an epi-
graph from Froebel -- "Come, let us live with our children" -- and
urges the teacher into Emersonian self-reliance: "Take joy in your
school; be a child with your children; show them your <u>dog</u>, your <u>cat</u>;
be, in turn, John and Mary and Kate and Frank; go wading in a creek;
have a birthday -- it is such fun! In other words, hitch this little
primer-wagon to the star of your own love and experience, and the
sure reward of high endeavor will be yours and theirs."

This, then, has brought us to the genesis of Dick and Jane. Like the
<u>Country</u> <u>Life</u> moonlight primer for adults, the 1909 <u>Child</u> <u>Classics</u>
primer is rural, comfortably nestled between the material referents
of Froebel's method and the transcendental stars and wagons of Ralph
Waldo Emerson, and supported by the firm shorings of familiar nursery
tales and jingles.

I should hasten to say that the works that I have analyzed were probably not the specific influences on Scott, Foresman Company, although
many of the more than one thousand primary readers I have examined
at the Center for Research libraries on the University of Chicago
campus were the gifts of the late Dr. William S. Gray, who as a professor at Chicago and chief consultant for Scott, Foresman and Company, was probably the twentieth-century equal to William Holmes
McGuffey in "teaching America how to read." Scott, Foresman is
not loose with its sales figures, but it has estimated that two out of
three adults in America learned to read with its readers -- the Elson-
Gray readers and then the Basic Reading Series -- both of which include
the characters Dick and Jane. Dr. Gray, in other words, was a leader,
but he was also familiar with all approaches to primary reading, world-
wide, and was obviously influenced by some of them.

Why then the long gestation and tardy births of Dick and Jane? Why

did all the antecedents fail to win popularity? And why should their entrance upon the scene cause such immediate acceptance? One reason can be to say that Scott, Foresman is the IBM of elementary education publishing, and it is a leader in secondary and college publishing as well, in certain fields. Like IBM, Scott, Foresman stresses research, quality control, continuous refinement of products and above all, "software" -- excellent teacher's aids, workbooks, audio-visual materials, such as wall charts and "big book" facsimiles for classroom work. Its sales staff is made up largely of successful former teachers. Also, like IBM, Scott, Foresman's spirit of adventure is a conservative spirit. The smaller companies who do not choose to compete by copying must become the leaders in bold innovation.

Until 1927, the Elson-Gray readers were anthologies in form, with some stories about children, but mainly relying upon the "sure appeal" classics. The pervasiveness of this approach during the period was documented in 1930 by Ruth Streitz and Dorothy Gradolf in an article in Childhood Education. In this study, twenty-nine first-grade readers were examined -- preprimers, primers, first readers. Eighteen of these published between 1910 and 1923 showed great duplication of classic folktales, while those published between 1924 and 1929 (a period coinciding with the publication dates on several "realistic" readers analyzed above) showed less duplication. The investigators disregarded story titles to allow for the underlying themes (as in the Lincoln Reader's "Billy Boy" version of the gingerbread boy story). Here is a brief summary of their findings:

The boy and the goat . . . . 12 versions among the
                                                        29 readers
Gingerbread boy . . . . 9 versions
Three pigs . . . . 9 versions
Henny penny . . . . 9 versions
Mouse's tail . . . . 9 versions
Little red hen . . . . 7 versions

Streitz and Gradolf concluded that while repetition of words is desirable, teachers often use several primers as supplementary readers and the repetition of plots serves no educational purpose. The children, they stated, "especially . . . like stories which recount the

experiences of other children, identifying themselves with these
incidents or reliving some of their own."

The writing was on the wall for publishers of fairy-tale primers, and
Scott, Foresman was ready to revise, having experimented with a
normal family approach in a small blue paper-backed "hand-chart"
printed in response to the needs of one-room school teachers who
could not afford the wall space for a large wall chart. "The mother"
and "the father" appear on the first two pages, and on the third page:
"This is the boy." It is Dick, but he is to remain nameless and sister-
less until 1930; and with curly black hair until 1940. The Hand Chart
continues conventionally with the "Little Red Hen." The 1930 Elson
PrePrimer is given over to the family of Dick, Jane, and Baby, who
is not named Sally for nearly twenty years. In 1936 Dick and Jane
is the title of the Basic PrePrimer. In 1940, the PrePrimer is We Look
and See, Dick has brown straight hair, his face is squarer, his sox
drooping and he wears tennis shoes. The family kitten, "Little Mew,"
is renamed "Puff." Another revision in 1951; then, in 1962, everyone
grows older, blue jeans appear. Finally, in 1965 a multi-ethnic version is made available, with black children, Penny and Mike, and
their parents.

In 1971, the continuing family stories were abandoned. Pressure from
Indians, Puerto Ricans, Chicanos, ghetto blacks, orientals and women
charging sexism made the creation of a "typical American family" with
which children could identify and relive experiences of their own a
task that required a Walt Whitman, not a primer. Besides, the controlled vocabulary, the famous "Thorndike" list of frequently used
words that had been the bastion of all American reading instruction
for more than half a century was being seriously challenged by modern
linguistic research. Children possess very large speaking and listening
vocabularies by the time they are in first grade. Why hold them to
"Run, Dick, run," "See Sally," "Oh, oh, oh!?" The 1971 revisions
were total, and Dick and Jane were no more.

Such is the history of Dick and Jane, and a partial explanation of
their popularity. They were followers. They followed the twenty-
year-old trend toward realism, and they followed the movement from
farm to city -- small city or suburb -- that was the demographic trend
of the twentieth century. They were the progeny of an excellent

publishing house. Yet none of these really explains the appeal to
children. That is probably a result of popular arts. The illustrations,
from the 1927 Hand Chart on, were brightly colored, and rather than
being up-cult sentimental pictures of adult ideals of children, they
were more realistic -- like child movie stars rather than Hummel
figures. Further, they really did move. The stories were in the pictures, the text provided the words which might be spoken by the
character. For example, in the 1930 edition, one of the first illustrations shows father, Dick and Jane running toward the house, away
from the reader. This illustration is to other primer art as seventeenth-
century baroque illusionist ceiling painting is to high Renaissance
frescos, explosive rather than serene. The analogy is extreme, I will
admit. Possibly a better comparison would be with action comic strips,
where the story is in the picture, and the words are dramatic rather
than narrative or explanatory.

It is vain to attempt to assert a direct relationship between comics
and primers, however. The Sesame Street and Electric Company
television phenomena are remarkable in primary education because
of their conscious and open philosophy of "if you can't lick 'em,
join 'em," which led to the direct use of techniques derived from
television commercials and Saturday morning cartoons and late afternoon slapstick reruns. Indeed, to a very considerable degree the
Pestalozzi-Froebel school of realistic relevance has been very slow
to respond to the child's world of popular mass culture. Disregarding
textbooks published after 1970, it appears that there have only been
some two or three primers that directly evolved from cartoon or comic-
strip art styles. The earliest was undoubtedly successful, for N. M.
Banta's The Brownie Primer was originally published in 1905 by the
A. Flanagan Company of Chicago but was newly reprinted without
apparent revision in 1935. The Bantas (N. Moore Banta and Alpha
Banta Benson) wrote many popular children's books -- The Bluebird
Book, Daffydowndilly and the Golden Touch among them -- but The
Brownie Primer is a true primer, with a controlled word-list and gradual development from short, highly repetitive texts to pages without
pictures. Curiously, the authors give no credit to Palmer Cox, the
Canadian writer who "invented" Brownies, "imaginary little sprites"
whose busy little world he illustrated in delightful cartoons and verses
for the St. Nicholas Magazine, from 1870 on. His books sold millions,
and a play, Palmer Cox's Brownies, ran five years on the stage at the

end of the century. Banta's Brownies are identical to Cox's. It is reasonable to assume, however, that teachers used The Brownie Primer as a supplementary book, much as Cowboy Sam books were used in the 1950's.

While not strictly based on a comic or on previously created character, Edna Walker Chandler's Cowboy Sam builds upon a "sure appeal" popular phenomenon, the western adventure. "Shorty," Sam's side-kick provides a summary of the book:

> "You did good work," said Shorty.
> "You shot the Black Wolf.
>   You found water.
> You shot two snakes.
> You took care of Dandy." [Sam's snakebitten horse.]

Move, over, gingerbread man! It is understandable that the Cowboy Sam series became immediately popular; since the folk tales had been phased out of primers during the depression years, the greatest degree of adventure available to little children through sanctioned printed words was squirting a puppy with a garden hose. Even so, Cowboy Sam appeared closer to reality than to fantasy. He performed no superhuman feats and his animals do not speak or think. Like the visual reality of the Dick and Jane illustrations, Sam's actions are closer to action movie ideal than to an imaginative otherworldly ideal. The appeal of the popular culture approach is particularly apparent when it is realized that the publishers illustrated Cowboy Sam in simple two-color sketchy drawings -- Cowboy Sam is two decades behind the other primers in its use of dull yellow and red-orange as the sole colors.

Between the Brownies and Cowboy Sam there is only one direct use of popular culture methods based on comic strips, although Anna Dorothea Cordts does not admit to it at any point in her New Path to Reading Series (1929). Dr. Cordts' method teaches words by the use of four-panel action strips, with the spoken words enclosed in rectangular "balloons," connected to the speaker by a line. The characters are continuous, but none are named. The drawings are in a comic strip style (the boy looks much like Winnie Winkle's brother Perry) with a minimum of details that might tend to obscure the essential

action.

Dr. Cordts' approach to the teaching of reading was startlingly unique, but even with the support of one of the most respected book publishers, Ginn and Company of Boston, hers appears to have been a dead-end venture. Even today, no one else seems to have capitulated to comic-strip balloons, regardless of the fact that at least up to the advent of television, newspaper comics and comic books probably constituted the bulk of young Americans' reading matter. Lest we grow impatient with the schools for not surrendering to the popular press, though, it might be noted that the phenomenon of the Big Little Books of the Whitman Publishing Company of Racine, Wisconsin appears to owe much to elementary textbook design.

If Scott, Foresman is the IBM of elementary textbook publishing, Whitman is the Woolworth's of juvenile reading and has probably been a greater force for extensive book reading than any other institution outside of public schools and libraries. Not only do Trixie Belden mysteries continue to emanate from Whitman, but the pulp paper gift classics -- Dickens, Spyri, Stevenson, Doyle, etc. -- found in dime stores are usually published by Whitman. Whitman, now one of the subsidiaries of Western Publishing Company, which also owns the equally popular if more prestigious Golden Press, developed Big Little Books in 1933 as comic "pick-ups." In format, they are like fat school readers, with an action picture on the right page and a narrative in large type on the left. The pictures provide the bare bones of the story (often with "flip-art" in the page corner) in later books, with a brief caption beneath, while the text duplicates the story in an "uncontrolled" vocabulary. Thus, the 1934 Buffalo Bill and the Pony Express, by Leon Morgan, illustrated by "Hal Arbo of the W Lazy S Ranch," begins:

> Bill Cody walked down the main street in Leavenworth, Kansas, gazing at the frame buildings on either side, mostly cheap one-story affairs with false fronts to give the impression of magnificent size.

Comic pick-ups were the mainstay, especially those drawn from the Chicago Tribune syndicate -- Dick Tracy, Orphan Annie, Terry and the Pirates -- although movies were rendered into novel form as well.

As a child, I learned of many silent picture cowboy stars such as Buck Jones and Ken Maynard from Big Little Books. Radio serial shows, too, were novelized, as with Jack Armstrong and Captain Midnight. During the first fifteen years of television, from 1949 to 1964, Big Little Books disappeared, but since then they have returned, many in reprints from earlier years, others capitalizing on television cartoon shows and adventure shows such as The Man from U.N.C.L.E. The current editor of these books, a former high school English teacher, reports of teachers in Chicago who use Big Little Books as remedial primers.

The Chicago teachers' practice is a notable foreshadowing of the new directions in primary reading training. Today, primary reading stories are complete in a single, heavily illustrated volume, providing a feeling of accomplishment as each book is finished, which certainly is one of the appeals of the Big Little Book. The vocabulary corresponds to the pictures and yet builds on the large recognition vocabulary which one acquires through listening to conversations, radio and television. The illustrations are as totally unrealistic as Bugs Bunny or The Flintstones, if the text does not require realism. Thus, in Scott, Foresman's new primer, The Bus Ride, the illustrations of monkeys, hippopatami and other animals all piling onto a bus are rendered in the spontaneous style of a child's poster-paint or finger-paint picture, while speed is indicated by the comic-art methods of using motion-lines and showing the bus with all four wheels off the ground as it tops a hill. This is not the only style used in the new primers of several of the major publishers. Some are in the Hummel-figure sweetness of Maurice Sendak, others are ultra-realistic, still others are in the manner of photographs of puppets, such as Whitman and Golden were using for pre-school story books in the 1950s.

Once again, it must be cautioned that there are probably no one-for-one reciprocal influences between textbook publishing and commercial popular entertainment publishing. That is, there is no evidence to suggest that Big Little Books "copied" primer design, nor that Anna Dorothea Cordts "copied" Winnie Winkle. And, The Brownie Primer is more akin to the "Dr. Seuss" reading readiness controlled vocabulary ventures of the 1960s (The Cat in the Hat, etc.) than it is to a new development in textbook techniques. Indeed, the evidence of my investigation appears to indicate that best-selling primer design is in a straight developmental line among professional textbook writers, editors, illustrators and publishers. Popular juvenile entertainment, on the other hand, appears to exist in a complicated network of popular phenomena, as for example, in the Big Little Books developing as a transition between series novels (Tom Swift, Hardy Boys) and comic books (starting in 1938) with plots, illustrations and characters drawn from popular film, newspaper strips, radio serials and film cartoons. In addition to textbooks and popular mass entertainment, there is a third area of juvenile publishing, which might be best referred to as children's literature. This is the library and trade book domain where the highest goals are Newberry Medals, Caldecott Awards and National Book Awards. Here the anonymity of textbooks and "pop" books is replaced by names such as Beatrix Potter, Marjorie Flack, Maud and Miska Petersham, Walter Brooks, Laura Ingalls Wilder, Robert Lawson, E. B. White, Maurice Sendak, Dr. Seuss, Arthur Rackham, Fritz Kredel, Lynd Ward and many others whose writing and artwork often crosses between children's and adult literatures.

Separated developmental lines, yes. But all three lines--textbook; pop book and children's literature exploit the same market of mass society. The actual taste, desires and preferences of children are always elusive; in point of fact, it is only very recently in world history that society has cared to inquire into whether children are anything other than creatures of putty to be molded forcibly into what is most convenient to the adult establishment. Just one generation before Pestalozzi, Jean-Jacques Rousseau, in Emile, "discovered" children as human beings, but we need only read the novels of Charles Dickens to be reminded that childhood education yielded very slowly to more humane concepts about teaching and learning. In America the democratization of elementary education is as old as the nation, but the production of popular materials to fit the interests of the child awaited the development of steam presses, lithography and linotype, all of which made possible cheap mass produced books. Alice in Wonderland appeared in 1865 in England, Little Women in 1868, Thomas Bailey Aldrich's Story of A Bad Boy in 1870, Tom Sawyer in 1876. The years directly following the Civil War also saw the popular works of Horatio Alger, Jr. and Dime Novels, and as the century went on the nation saw the development of normal schools with Colonel Parker's American versions of Froebel's methods, and,

in art education, of Louis Prang, who operated an art education school and published colored lithographs and sold wooden drawing models and paints for primary art experiences. In other words, all three branches of publication directed toward a children's market developed only during the past century, almost simultaneously, in children's literature and illustration, in popular entertainment literature, and in educational materials with child interest as a paramount consideration.

Brilliantly colored primers appear at least as early as 1899, when Gertrude Anderson Alexander of the Peabody Normal College of Nashville produced First Step in Reading. Some of the colors did not register perfectly, but nonetheless it would be nearly thirty years before such brightness of color, naturalism and such high good humor would reappear in the Elson-Gray readers and their imitators, and it would be nearly three-quarters of a century before such respect for the experience of children would be shown as Alexander implies in her "Hints for Teachers." She begins, "When a child enters school he knows the names of common objects; he recognizes the words when he hears them; and he can intelligently use these words in speech to express his thoughts. The teacher then should build upon this foundation. . . . The order of the work should therefore begin with conversation. . . . Comparatively little poetry has been introduced, because poetry is hard reading for children." (Heresy!) The primer ends with "The Three Pigs," where the comic, rapidly drawn black-and-white illustrations have a ribald drama closer to Walt Disney's art than to any primers prior to 1970. Even a phonics lesson is rendered in a frenzy of activity with dialogue "balloons" emanating from various mouths in a single cartoon: a naughty dog growls "r, r, r" as two arched and fluffed cats say "f, f, f" and "th, th, th" a bee hovers above, "z, z, z;" a cow looks over a fence with moral expression, and ruminates "m, m, m," and a boy and girl rush to the rescue variously saying "s, s, s" and "sh, sh, sh" to the animals. There is more: First Steps in Reading also included photographic reproductions of paintings in the academic style of the day.

The point of this is that from quite early the writers and publishers of elementary school books were drawing upon the latest technical advances in printing and upon some of the methods of popular publishing. The reproduction of a painting in a book by means of half-tone

photography, for example, was not developed into a mass process
until about 1890, but it was quickly tried in this primer as a method
of achieving greater realism and immediacy. Five years later, in
1904, The Outdoor Primer of Eulalie Osgood Grover, published by
Rand McNally press, was based on the belief that children, "in
repeating the history of the race, find their chief interests and their
most natural activities in the wide out-of-doors," and so "the lessons
are based upon the actual life of actual children, and upon child
and animal life as depicted in famous paintings. Nothing but photographs from life and paintings have been used as illustrations, which
adds to the sense of reality in the book." Well, hardly. The reproductions are muddy, and the photographs are rather awkwardly posed
views of children squinting into the sunlight; but then, twenty-five
years later, a similar attempt at photographic realism in At The Farm
is just as drab, in spite of the further device of carrying real-life
continuing characters to the extreme of assuring the readers that
"these are true stories about a real Bob and a real Nancy who had
many good times having their pictures taken and did all of the
things the stories tell about." Real Bob and real Nancy and the
author are real Texans and the stories take place on a cattle ranch,
but the effect is neither so adventurous as Cowboy Sam nor so bright
as Dick and Jane.

The various attempts at winning the interest of children to primers are
only partially motivated by respect for children, but at least an equal
motivation is the size of the potential market for book sales. Although
my discussion has been limited to primers, it is often true that the
primer sets the pattern for adopting a whole six-grade reading series,
and the elementary school population in 1970 was considerably in
excess of twenty-five million pupils. The potential for the sales of
primers in a given year is probably close to one million volumes. The
children's attention is well worth getting and holding. It is therefore
not a mere matter of publishing the most efficient, consistent and
economical tool for teaching reading, which might be the case if the
United States had only universal compulsory education, but the United
States has universal compulsory education and local control and a free
enterprise profit-motivated publishing industry. Popularity matters.

Elementary school publishing is unquestionably a popular art in its
attempts to woo its peculiar audience, an audience which is assembled

84

under compulsion, an audience with no buying power, an audience with scheduled impermanence. It is for this audience that the devices of popular entertainment are tried and incorporated: bright colors, real-life realism, puppets, popular cartoon and comic styles and subjects, humor, animals of fact and fancy. So far as the children are concerned, this just about ends the popular arts of the primer. But it does not end the competition for the popular audience, for primers are selected by teachers and school officials, and, less directly, by American communities.

In this way, primers and other schoolbooks reflect popular values and tastes. These have always been establishment values, the values of the dominant majority of the time. As a matter of fact, it would be an entirely tenable thesis to state that the best-selling primers of any time in American history express in mythic simplicity the predominant culture of the day. This statement even includes those primers of the 1960s, still current, that include "minority" figures and civil rights parables. Today most of us are surprised not to see black models in mail order catalogs or black people in television commercials. And in comics, on cereal boxes, in children's literature, "multiethnic" pictures are commonplace. They represent the dominant values of the society. There is no denying that the dominant view lagged behind radicals and progressives, but what is an <u>avant garde</u> without a mass to lag behind it? The dominant place of urban life in the United States was not reflected in best-selling primers until the 1930s, despite the fact that by 1920 more than half the population lived in urban areas. It is true that this statement is based on the standard of 2500 persons as the statistical transition figure between rural and urban, which may seem ridiculously small to metropolitan residents, but the size of the community is nowhere so significant in primerland as is the lifestyle distinction between farm and non-farm. To put these differences into the words of folk-wisdom, the cliche of "it's a nice place to visit, but I wouldn't want to live there" provides a key to interpreting popular values in primers. Pay attention to what place is visited, and what place is home, and you will have a picture of what is the dominant environmental value. A review of some of the primers discussed earlier will support this. The 1909 Child Classics was entirely rural. In 1917, the <u>Kendall Primer's</u> Bob and Betty traveled from their small town to the city. In the 1926 <u>Lincoln Reader</u>, Billy Boy and Betty Girl visit grandfather's farm, and this continues as a pattern up through the Second World War, after which the "return of the native" to a family farm gradually succumbs to the coalescing of family farms into large, impersonal agri-industrial units. There are even more pointed instances, from the Country Life reader of 1915 (essentially a minority reader for poor farmers) where readers are admonished not to miss the "joy of country life," to the 1924 Laidlaw Primer where Tom's curiosity about the wooden farm house leads to a noticeably apologetic tone in Grandfather's "We have an old house. . . . The brick chimney is old, too. . . . Grandmother and I like it here. We like to live on a farm." The bleak Hemingway style produces a plaintive conflict in values in these few pages -- Grandfather, wistful about the fast car, setting forth apples and milk as rural inducements, but Father brusquely interrupting: "What time is it, Mother? It is time to go home now. Come children, we shall go."

The primers express the middle mass values; there is no other way. Minority readers are born frequently, but they will exist only while the majority will tolerate them. In 1938, for example, Emma E. Akin of Drumright, Oklahoma wrote the Negro American Series, with photographic illustrations including some Oklahoma black shanties. This is not a primer, but its approach is basically middle-class and pastoral, with activities taking place in a New Deal-supported WPA school. The Country Life primer is a minority reader, too, but it is essentially establishment-oriented toward progressive scientific agriculture. But woe betide the local community that goes against the dominant values, as Twin Lakes, Wisconsin found in 1961 when it lost a reactionary rebellion, after attempting to replace Dick and Jane and sight reading with McGuffey's morality and phonics. Americans watched with nostalgic amusement, but the crushing and inevitable victory of the Wisconsin State Department of Public Instruction was softened only by the permission to use as a "reference book" the outdated readers that had dominated American education for eighty-four years from 1836 to 1920, amassing total sales of 122 million textbooks.

But the "tyranny" of the middle-class tastes is not directed toward promoting the lowest common denominator. Schooling is taken seriously by our citizens, and quite rightly so. The cultural values expressed by the school and the textbooks are the best values of the

majority, or possibly, cynics might say, they are the "dress-up" values of the masses. People in primers always dress a little better than their real-life counterparts; their homes are a little bigger and neater than the average. Moreover, the artwork is always in the style of good popular arts. Most often it can be profitably compared with the advertisements and commercial art that derive from the current vogue. Without repeating the analysis above, I would call attention to the aesthetic tags that I have applied to illustrations: Pre-Raphaelite, William Morris, academic painting, Tiffany, art nouveau, art deco. Very rarely have primers been illustrated in a strictly popular tradition (the Brownies and Cowboy Sam), and I have found only one that is frivolous: the Goober Village primer of 1936, wherein a "Dick and Jane" family is made up of peanuts, yea, even unto peanut kittens. Not surprisingly, the readers of the 1930s have illustrations that follow the style of the calendar art genre artists, who in turn, were in the regionalist traditions of John Steuart Curry, Thomas Hart Benton, and Grant Wood. Even closer parallels exist with the better magazine illustrations, such as appeared in the Saturday Evening Post. Probably the ideal instance from the 1930s is Row Peterson's Alice and Jerry Books (1936). The colors are bright; each story has an attractive page border in a single color. The idyllic seacoast village is always in bloom. Backgrounds are simple, or in many cases, non-existent, with the figures set on the plain page. In 1948 the page borders, which looked like shelf paper, anyway, were dispensed with. The children now are shown in complete paintings, and the hint of bounding outlines of 1936 are gone, making the illustrations less like a coloring book. The village houses become more realistic, larger and more densely ranged. The overall prosperity is more noticeable, the realism, like that of magazine illustrations of the forties, greater. Similar changes occurred in the Dick and Jane series. Up until 1940 the primers had "coloring-book" outlines. In 1940 they were more obviously painted with more naturalistic shading. Whereas the earlier backgrounds were in an art deco style--stylized like pastel stage scenery -- after 1940 the backgrounds contain interesting and colorful details. In 1962, the entire style is bolder and more painterly. Overall, the illustrations of the Forties become more photographic in content, but freer in brushwork.

The next two decades, of course, posed a problem. Abstract expressionism, then pop and op painting could do nothing for books dedicated

to real life stories; while comics and Walt Disney were too popular, too fanciful and too "uncultured" to emulate. Those magazines to survive the period cut out fiction and realistic illustration. Advertisements went "mod." Children's literature, however, became big business during the post-war baby boom and illustrators went in all stylistic directions. The predominant children's literature styles, however, followed either cartoon traditions from Walt Disney's bold-colored, flat, naturalistic, stylized work of the Snow White period to the sophisticated reactions to Disney such as the simplified line drawings of Gerald McBoing-Boing and the Nearsighted Mr. Magoo; or they were in the spontaneous painterly vogue of Raoul Dufy; or they revived sentimental adult pleasures with big-eyed doll-children. One thing is sure: the photographic reporting of reality that continued to characterize all primers was rarely employed in either popular children's arts or in children's literature.

Something had to "give," with so much aesthetic descrepancy between primer realism and establishment expressionism. By the 1960s, realistic art was not just old hat, it was embarrassingly lower class. Even discount and dime store sported Feininger imitations, safe Braques and slapdash Dufys. What "gave," as everyone knows, was neither art nor aesthetic, but social values and picture content. In the briefest analysis, the community still said "we want reality, but your primer reality is a fairy tale." America at last discovered that primers teach more than how-to-read.

The discovery of how many social values were implied by primers came as a shock. The shock to primary grade teachers and to editors of primers, however, was to find that the community was shocked. After all, educators knew that values were implied in the readers. They had put them there. The absence of some values -- ethnic, religious, regional, metropolitan -- were hardly anything other than the established American way: try to find published collections of major American writers and artists prior to 1965 that included Countee Cullen, Ralph Ellison, Charles White, Oscar Howe. They are as scarce as adolescent big brothers in a primer, and that is as scarce as hen's teeth. In 1954 the first attack on reader content demonstrated that scarity unequivocally. Many popular journalistic attacks would follow, but Abraham Tannenbaum's "Family Living in Textbook Town" in Progressive Education of March, 1954 contains the essence of all

that they would say. Tannenbaum's method was like that of the two
investigators who in 1930 had reversed the trend from fantastic folk
tales to everyday reality by demonstrating the boring repetition of
certain tales. Tannenbaum conducted a quantitative analysis of
1084 illustrations in first, second and third grade readers published
in the decade 1943-1953. Here is a partial summary of his findings:

Number of illustrations showing a family of two or three children	465
Number of illustrations showing a family of four children	6
Number of illustrations showing a family of more than four children	0
Adolescent or adult brothers or sisters appear	0
Color or ethnic groups living in textbook town	0
Slums in textbook town	0
Family living in city apartment or flat	1
Family living in suburban-style home	190
Mother shows evidence of outside occupation	0
Mother smiles or is obviously contented	217
Mother is angry, sad, worried	6
Father smiles or is obviously contented	151
Father is angry, sad, worried	4

Abraham Tannenbaum's analysis of his statistics are especially interesting in the light of the 1930s report of Streitz and Gradolf, and in
the light of the thirty-year struggle to achieve "textbook town." He
concludes, "Textbook Town, with its bland style of living, is nothing
more than an idealized middle-class community where characters are
mere shadows, and where nothing exciting or of real importance ever
happens. To the lower-class child it looms as a 'never-never' world
that may excite in him vague dreams of attainment, but which will
probably elude him forever. He finds it only slightly less improbable
than the fairyland he encounters in fables, except that the plots and
characters in the latter type of literature are far more memorable."

In 1930, primers had been urged to tell of the real experience of
other children; twenty-four years later such attempts were condemned
as a bland world of fancied reality. Ten years after that primers
revised themselves by holding up a mirror to Textbook Town reality

again, only this mirror was a little larger, a little more brightly polished. But what it reflected was the same Town with the neighborhood tipped by some very presentable "ethnics." During the same time, Americans were witnessing brutal realities on television at one moment, and "greening of America" escapes from reality at the next. The brutal realities were readily available to children from the popular media, and so the primers began, slowly, in the early 1970s, to edge toward safer unreality. The pendulum was swinging.

And it will continue to swing. It is the way of American education to change in response to a network of influences, not all of which are harmonious. Reading educational theory is one of those influences, but even that is at war with itself. In a totalitarian nation, the only important influence other than educational theory would be governmental policy. In the United States, however, this is limited to an indirect influence, as in the case of civil rights legislation and court decisions forcing shifts in public opinion, and thereupon, changes in textbooks. Local influences are far more important than national influences, and this is one way that the various publishers in America survive, for in our middle-class society, the local and regional differences are subtle. A slight variation in scenery, hair color, or home furnishings may assure a book sale in one community and not even consideration in another. Some states will make statewide text adoptions and it can be well worth the expense for a publisher to prepare a book to regional specifications and hope for some other sales out-of-state. But such regional differences are far more likely to become manifest in social studies books (such as the causes of the Civil War) or biology (evolution), for older students, than they are in primers.

Primers are introductions to <u>national</u> values, not provincial values. Provincial values are what every first grader brings from his home and what he must rid himself of. If he does not, he will become a cultural cripple such as those that Cora Wilson Stewart dedicated herself to normalize in moonlight schools. As I stated at the outset, her <u>Country Life</u> primer did this more directly than any child primers, because she could aim her normal correctives at real and salient aberrations, while the producers of children's primers must anticipate and prevent possible deviations from the norm, but in a general way, because there are no specific deviations that can apply to six-year-olds.

Thus, for over a century, the American method has been to present to children, in positive terms, a summary of normal behavior. Self-reliance and family responsibility: The Little Red Hen. The danger of too much individualism: The Gingerbread Boy. Industry and the work ethic: The Three Little Pigs. And so on. Dick and Jane's value training is not revolutionary in purpose, regardless of how revolutionary its realistic aesthetic was. The realistic primers were the Studs Lonigan of the six-year set, entirely appropriate to the prevailing aesthetics of the Thirties and Forties.

The same norms are taught today, with a little brotherhood and find-your-individualism-in ethnic-heredity mixed in. These are positive norms for a crowded country that no longer admits floods of extremely different foreigners. In earlier days absolute individualism as a way of building one's house of bricks was valued; wrenching foreigners into an approximate of the "normal" American was a fulfillment for those foreigners; but now we must live so close together that our inescapable subtle differences will surface and we must learn to accept ourselves and others through understanding these differences. This too is "the American way," the norm to which our children must measure up for survival and success in the remainder of this century, as surely as the moonlight farmers needed checkbooks and crop rotation for survival and success in the beginning of the century.

And it really doesn't much matter to the child whether the norms are inculcated in reality or in fantasy -- either way, the values are real dreams, ideals that we follow as if they were true. Reality or fantasy is probably a matter of taste, the adult's more than the child's, and taste means aesthetics. The aesthetic of the primer is the aesthetic of the marketplace, the democratic mass marketplace, the same marketplace that all American popular arts serve. Thus, popular influences must be included among those that swing the educational pendulum. Direct influences and causal relationships between popular culture and normal primers may be impossible to demonstrate, but there are significant parallels and coincidences. For example, prior to the 1930s when beginning reading in schools was largely fanciful, popular children's literature was realistic -- Tom Swift and heroes of his ilk required little suspension of disbelief -- but within a few years after American children began to cut their literary teeth on the middle-class realism of Dick and Jane, Walt Disney's talking

animals and the comic hero, <u>Superman</u> (1938) rose to such popularity that they threatened the security of establishment aesthetic standards. Notwithstanding their safe and proper morality, both Disney and the superhuman comic book stories showed the faces of evil and death in mythic fancies. Parents of the three decades may have taken their children to see the fancies and violence of <u>The Three Little Pigs</u>, <u>Snow White</u>, <u>Pinocchio</u>, <u>Dumbo</u> and other <u>Disney films</u>, and everyone may have applauded Donald Duck, Bugs Bunny, and Woody Woodpecker, but these did not find their ways into the readers in either content or style. Parents and educators may have sustained a continuing war against unrealistic and cheap cartoons and comic books, but the children continued to buy, read, swap, and read some more comic books.

Would it not be fair to suggest that children in their beginning reading experiences need a balance between reality and fancy, not as a matter of taste, but as a necessity for mental development; not as an expression of the norm, but as an expression of deeply ingrained myths; and that when schools fail to supply one or the other, popular (or folk) traditions will satisfy the need? Might not it also be true that children are aware that there are flies in the soup of life, that there is evil, injustice and death in the world, and that these fearful truths must be expressed to be met and understood? The realistic primer never provided such expression in any forms -- no trolls, no witches, big bad wolves, ugly ducklings, mobsters or mean men down the block who won't let you take the short cut through their yards to the playground. The transitional moonlight <u>Country Life</u> primer provided such negatives as well as the positive values, but the realistic primers gave only positive norms of the American material and social ideal of perfection. To what degree modern primers will combine reality and fantasy, and positive and negative, will depend upon the interactions among the various influences on the educational pendulum, but regardless of the methods and aesthetics, the popular norm will be the message.

Until the Fifties when we all learned to be wary of admitting to conformity, teachers colleges were frankly called <u>normal schools</u>, after a French tradition of the <u>ecole normale</u>. There teachers-to-be learned how to instruct children consistently in the norms of society, science and cultivation. The overt intent of this kind of education

is made more clear from the etymotogy of <u>norm</u>, which originated in the norma, the carpenter's square. Therein will be found the right angle from which to view the world. Therein will be found the measure of one's rectitude, which measure is that of the dominant popular tastes. Therein will be found the norms expressed in the popular primers, at any time in our cultural history; and, like it or not, they are always a little big square.

The Democratic Yard
and Garden

Walt Whitman, as we all know, is the Democratic Poet, despite the
fact that he has never won popularity among the democratic masses.
His popularity remains as it began; he is still the darling of the intel-
ligentsia around the globe. His theories and experiments in language,
subject matter and prosody were all directed toward the common man,
who Whitman regarded as a transcendental hero. Edgar Allen Poe,
on the other hand, was a wiser American poet in regard to the popular
audience. He knew, as he lucidly and coolheadedly set forth in
"The Philosophy of Composition," what the popular mind really wanted:
a short narrative, a minimum of metaphor, clear rhyme, and easily
discernable meter, and a "universally appreciable" topic within the
"legitimate province" of poetry. Almost like a modern advertising
firm of Madison Avenue, Poe analyzed the effect wanted, explained
the means of achieving that effect, and thereupon wrote the poem -
which is "The Raven," a sure-fire winner if ever there was one.

Whitman's democratic talent was not for the market place, however.
He was a reporter with that rare commodity, a heart overflowing with
love for humanity and all that humankind live and use and say. Unlike
Poe, he saw and listened to the people, but also, unlike Poe, he

thought that the people <u>valued</u> what they lived, and used and said, and would recognize it as art, or at least, as the raw material for art. The popular mind, though, separates the "legitimate province" of art from the everyday province of life, where song, dance, decorations and "pretties" are either adjuncts of social functions, like weddings, or entertainment, like card games. For the popular mind, Art <u>qua</u> (popular) Art, is exotic, venerable and aristocratic. In brief, to the popular mind, art should be no more like life than Sunday is like Thursday. Thursday art is indeed a transcendental thing, for it is all in the eye of the beholder, an eye cleared of conventional scales, glaze, ennui and tedium; an eye which looks not for Sunday best and florist's orchids, but which discerns the loveliness of Thursday's string beans and April's lilacs.

> "In the dooryard fronting an old farm-house near the white-wash'd palings, stands the lilac-bush tall-growing with heart-shaped leaves of rich green, with many a pointed blossom rising delicate, with the perfume strong I love, with every leaf a miracle -- and from this bush in the door yard, with delicate-color'd blossoms and heart-shaped leaves of rich green, a sprig with its flower I break."

It is that door yard, that farmhouse, that fence of palings, and that lilac-bush, all of which I draw from Whitman's superb elegy on the death of Abraham Lincoln, "When Lilacs Last in the Dooryard Bloom'd," that will serve as <u>genius loci</u> for this discussion of the democratic garden and its environs and denizens, the sundry <u>putti</u>, <u>amphorae</u>, planters, spring-necked flamingos, plastic mushrooms, and bleach-bottle birdhouses that populate and afflict the gardens of America. The garden images of Whitman's elegy are rural and of the mid-nineteenth century, and to that extent may seem remote to urban-suburban contemporary America, but even where the modern popular garden does not derive directly from rural or small-town mid-America of a century past, it develops from some particularly American requisites, which are the privately owned home, the front yard, high labor costs, the home handyman, and the network of popular mass-distributed knowledge and materials as they have been embodied in how-to-do-it publications and in the mail-order catalog.

Traditionally, in American studies, we turn to Andrew Jackson

Downing as the prophet and purveyor of landscape gardening, and to his brother in monogram, Alexander Jackson Davis, as the promoter of popular American cottage architecture. Of the two, Downing is the more significant for the democratic garden. Like the great designer of the eighteenth century English aristocratic garden, "Capability" Brown, Andrew Jackson Downing started humbly enough, as a gardener and nurseryman, but rapidly became the taste-maker for outdoor America in the 1840s. Even so, to take Andrew Jackson Downing in a straight dose as the prophet of American democratic garden art is somewhat mistaken. True, his Treatise on the Theory and Practice of Landscape Gardening Adapted to North America with a view to the Improvement of Country Residences (first edition 1841, subsequent editions through 1869) set patterns whose reverberations are still felt. As John O. Simonds, one of America's leading landscape architects, wrote in an introduction to a facsimile edition in 1967, "Downing's influence on American landscape planning was, and still is, immense. It was he who so compellingly established the principle of asymmetrical design in this country and thereby 'laid the foundation for a whole new sequence of experiments in planning and spatial organization.'"

Nonetheless, investigation into Downing's extremely interesting book will show that his is a democracy of the Rich. We must not be hoodwinked by the words "rural" and "cottage," for the only architectural illustrations in his book that will relate directly to popular economics are under the headings of "entrance lodges." Downing's clients were the wealthy homeowners of the lower Hudson - a heroic rural landscape that not all Americans will realize is virtually within sight of the skyscrapers of Manhattan - and, had not his life been cut short (heroically dying, while saving fellow-passengers following the explosion of the steamboat Henry Clay) in 1852, we might know him as the designer of the malls and grounds of the White House, the Capitol and the Smithsonian Institution. Compared to European landscape architects, he is indeed democratic, as his name seems to proclaim, and he was fully aware of the need to scale down. "In the United States," he wrote, "it is highly improbable that we shall ever witness such splendid examples of landscape gardens as those abroad. . . . Here the rights of man are held to be equal. . . . The number of individuals among us who possess wealth and refinement sufficient to enable them to enjoy the pleasures of a country

life. . . is every day increasing." From Downing's clients of wealth and refinement of "the Atlantic states" to transappalachian settler and, later, after 1862, to homesteaders, is not an impossible leap, but it is nevertheless the all-important difference between the cultivated class of leisure who can retain a landscape consultant and a corps of gardeners, and the popular class of laborers and farmers who must derive their arts from home-grown traditions or from the mass market.

Downing's democratic landscapes, therefore, need interpreting, simplifying, economizing and marketing for the families of America. Partly this is achieved informally by a singularly American process. On a Sunday drive we see a large home or garden we admire, and we set about imitating it, in materials, expense and expanse within our means, with a resultant provincialization that will at best be a genuinely new art style, and at worst, will be a reprehensible travesty. This casual Sunday imitation might be documented today by sociological survey, but for the most part, it is as elusive and irretrievable as all folk transmissions. It is, nonetheless, real, and may be the predominant mode of cultural change and exchange. As to the other modes of transmission as they relate to gardens, yards and landscape architecture, (they are almost exclusively printed media), more will develop in this chapter, but it might be best to start with some terminology and history.

The word garden is related to the word yard, both deriving from the concept of enclosed surroundings. Within the Teutonic tradition from which our language and dominant culture have developed, there is neither art nor decoration implied in these words. The garden as an aesthetic yard, however, has a long history, especially in the Near East (as in the Hanging Gardens of Babylon and in the Persian courtyard water gardens and such descendants as we would know from the Alhambra in Granada in Spain); in China (as in the Forbidden City of Peking); in Mexico (in the empire of the Inca and in the famous island and roof gardens of Tenochtlitan and Texcoco); and in ancient Rome (as in the descriptions by Pliny the Younger and in the reconstructions and murals of Pompeii). The great gardens of today are outgrowths of these antecedents, developing, as have most of the cultural goods and evils of the modern world, from the fifteenth century Renaissance in northern Italy and from the great age of

exploration which followed. First was the humanists' imitations of gardens and natural beauty as they understood them from Virgil's Georgics and Pliny's Letters, with all the emphasis upon symmetrical harmony and mathematical precision that the Renaissance classicists savored. Along with this was the associated literary-philosophical playing of Florentine and Roman patrons who revived the Groves of Academe for their new platonists. From the Orient and from the New World came horticultural splendors – from Persia, Whitman's democratic shrub, the lilac, around 1500; from Turkey, the tulip, which was destined to become the object of crazy speculation in the first of the international fads a century later; from Mexico, cannas, zinnias, amarylis, dahlias – and, mainstay of Grandma's border garden, nasturtiums. Eatables are outside our aesthetic province, but at the same time, from the New World came Irish potatoes, French beans, Italian tomatoes, Spanish peppers, Dutch chocolate and Indian corn.

Prior to the Renaissance, though, the edible plants in the garden were central, and so well as can be discerned from the documents of the middle ages, flowers were incidental, at best. Even rose bushes could be used for hedges, their petals eaten in salads or distilled into perfumes, and their hips cooked and eaten. According to Edward Hyams, the medieval garden plan for St. Gall in Switzerland listed roses and lilies as medicinals. But as this implies, the medieval garden was the prerogative of monastery and aristocracy. We are not to picture serfs and peasants setting out daffodils amid their black radishes, turnips and leeks. The settlement of the Americas, in other words, took place at the same time that European garden art was barely out of its renascent infancy. For the most part, however, the settlers were unaffected by the art of gardening, which was an aristocratic art. Indeed, there is practically no evidence to support the idea of a folk tradition of ornamental gardening or yardkeeping. "New England gardens during the first century following the settlements," Hyams says, "were very like English cottage and farmhouse gardens. Like them they had mixed flowers and vegetables, herbs and salads, usually in front and usually fenced or walled. . . . The flowers grown were a small selection of those chiefly grown in England. . .," lilies, peonies, gilly flowers, hollyhocks, while "marigold, poppy and saffron crocus were grown more for medicinal or culinary reasons than for ornament." Even this description might be debatable; folk gardens are not found in pictorial records, they do not lend themselves

98

to archaeological research, and while the annual cycle from seed to seed pod may be continuous, it is too impermanent to appear in wills or dowry records, wherein are found some records of everyday possessions of the late middle ages. Folksong abounds in horticultural allusion, but these, like the bower of roses by Bendemeer's stream, are sweet edens of dalliance outside the pale and palings of rural yards. It is reasonable, of course, to presume that the English popular garden of today may be the end-product of a continuous tradition dating from late medieval times, from which we could reconstruct or postulate such a garden as Hyams describes. Certainly the English popular garden - those riotous, topsy-turvey yard-sized window boxes that charm the American tourist - are ornamental from sheer abundance. In a little-known minor masterpiece of writing in the Emersonian tradition, the American landscape architect, Fletcher Steele, wrote in 1964 that for the Englishman "horticulture frankly takes precedence over design. . . . The places [the landscape architect] likes the best and believes most English show few signs of planning as he used the word. They just grow. They are the comfortable kingdom where the Englishman lives in his own way with what he cares for - his family, friends and servants, his animals and his plants. All are given place and none is allowed to interfere with the others." The English cult of privacy marks the main differentiating characteristic of the American yard and garden, and should show clearly that the English popular garden is the least of influences on America. Our yards, as Christopher Tunnard and Henry Hope Reed succinctly demonstrate, grew from the clearing, which expands outward; not from the wall, which contains inward.

In spite of these differences, England is a good starting place, not because of popular tradition, but for two other reasons. One reason, of which more later, is the aristocratic tradition. The other reason is socio-economic. The popular garden requires an independent middle-class, homeownership and a degree of wealth. Ornamenting one's surroundings is not an art for slave, serf or tenant. It is an announcement of pride and security of ownership, it is a recognition of a creative and contributing monument to leisure. When Americans feel their worth, they put down roots by design. A few years ago, when the oil-rich bachelors, masters and doctors of an Oklahoma city determined to help the black shackers on the other side of the tracks - near the smelting plant - they asked what they might do to

99

help, and the answer came back, "give us flower seeds." Similarly, when urban ghetto dwellers made "people's parks" out of vacant lots, they demonstrated pride, permanence and leisure. Derek Clifford, possibly the most comprehensive of modern historians of garden design, maintains that "All gardens are the product of leisure. It is no good looking for gardens in a society which needs all its energies to survive." Overwhelmingly, therefore, garden art has been a royal, aristocratic and monastic art, but writers on the subject have almost totally ignored the leisure gardens of the independent working middle-class. The independent yeoman farmer, though, has rarely indulged in ornamental horticulture. Plants are his business, not his pleasure. So we must look to the cities and towns.

Holland from the late sixteenth century throughout the seventeenth century provides the first clear instance of the middle-class ornamental garden. Of all the European peoples, the Dutch most clearly parallel the American value systems. Republican, mercantile, puritanistic, child-spoiling, home-loving and thoroughly materialistic, the Dutch proudly and lovingly recorded their well-being, their possessions, their familiar scenes in positivist painting, for those who could afford them, and in mass-produced etchings and engravings for those who could not afford original paintings. Home interiors, almost invariably with windows opened to a courtyard, landscapes of the four seasons and floral paintings all expressed the proud self-sufficiency, the pleasant leisure, and the great love of cultivated nature of the Dutch, in works of the masters and "little masters:" Vermeer, DeHooch, Steen, Van Ruisdael, Bosschaert, Avercamp, Van der Neer, Van de Velde and many others among them. Closer examination, though, will show that the Dutch gardens are in courtyards, not yards such as we know in America. The courtyard garden does appear in colonial and nineteenth century America, but not in the American mainstream. In the Southwest - in the old Governor's Palace in Santa Fe, for instance - the Spanish-Moorish tradition persists, while in New Orleans - the Court of the Two Sisters is one example - the French bourgeois tradition continues. Of that tradition, Fletcher Steele says, "The Frenchman does not care much for what the American reveres as Nature - irregular country and wide views. . . . He wants his vistas closed, his privacy complete." Of this, the "Happy Prison," Steele says, "Life in a bourgeois garden is not on guard. Slippers and dressing gown, bundles of letters,

an afternoon nap after kicking off one's shoes - a general sense of
freedom from intrusion by formal callers - make a place that is dear
to family life though not fitted to show snooping foreigners, whether
indoors or out."

These in-turning traditions of Dutch, Spanish and French are rarely
found in America today, even where houses are crowded into cities.
A ride on the "el" or along a freeway overpass or through the alleys
of a large American city shows not Happy Prisons, but little yards
whose only difference from the small-town and suburban yards is to be
found in the wooden fences that divide them from one another. The
only common exception (uncommon exceptions can always be found)
are the roof gardens of wealthy urbanites, (which are self-conscious
architect-designed "yards"), and the Japanese-inspired gardens
promoted by Sunset magazine for the west coast. Both are contrived
phenomena of the mid-twentieth century, and both have great potential for a future of urban renewal, high-rise retirement buildings, and
apartment houses.

Returning to the seventeenth-century Dutch paintings, it is interesting
to notice that in the rural scenes there are no yards or gardens around
buildings. In a number of cases the surroundings are full of such bucolic flotsam as tree trunks, decayed sheepfolds and cast-off implements. The banks of rural canals are especially strewn with such
debris. This may constitute a foreshadowing of America's litter and
rural junk piles, but it is probably more economic than ethnic in
origin, that is, it bespeaks of prosperity, not Netherlandish delight
in disorder. Junk will be one of the main threads of thought in this
chapter, so it would be appropriate here to remark upon the economic
significance of junk in the landscape.

In a fascinating, if partly tongue-in-cheek book, Farmer's Law: Junk
in a World of Affluence, Richard N. Farmer, chairman of the Department of International Business at Indiana University, constructs a
world-wide scale that relates "observable trash" to per capita gross
national product, and finds that junk is most visible at the two ends
of the economic scale. Where the per capita GNP is below $50,
(as in the South Pacific or the Arabian desert) trash is everywhere,
because none gets used. Where the income is $1201-2500, (as in
West Germany, the United Kingdom, Norway and Australia) trash

is also almost everywhere, because utilization by means of repair and recycling is made expensive by high labor costs. The cleanest nations, Farmer says, are those like India and Bolivia, in the $51-$200 bracket, where garbage is eaten, cars are totally stripped, bottles become glassware, tin cans are turned into shingles and household implements, and where everything is ingeniously converted. "Fishing out a Model T Ford axle from a dry creek to use as the main support of a homemade drill press is probably a lost art in the United States, but it still goes on abroad."

Junk is a far piece from the usual discussion of garden art and landscape design, and the topic may begin to suggest just how elusive the democratic garden is. As the foregoing implies, I am assuming that the lack of evidence of pre-nineteenth-century democratic or popular ornamental gardens represents an absence of the type. Such reasoning from negative evidence is never secure, because so very often all cultural evidence of a given time or place is funnelled - filtered is a better term - through the eyes, minds, hands and pens of an exclusive class which often does not deign to notice popular phenomena, and is sometimes quite blind to the ways of the preponderance of humanity. We need not point the finger of blame at the scribes and scholars of past generations alone. For all our liberalism and egalitarianism today, there is little attention paid to popular tastes beyond market surveys for the present generation, and even Professor Farmer's penchant for touring the scrapyards and garbage heaps of the world is reported with a tone of good-humored bravado.

The point that I am making is that the Dutch records of yards, gardens and litter may not really demonstrate the republican middle-class nature of their garden-culture so much as it is a reflection of a photographic style of genre painting that chose not to romanticize. I do not want to weaken my thesis, of course, but neither do I wish to wink at the complex problems of documenting popular phenomena of the past. Thus, while the earliest body of visual evidence of the American home yard will be found in the prints of Currier and Ives, the Currier and Ives prints constitute a gussied-up reality wherein the children are always clean, the sun is almost always shining, and the yards are clear of debris. We all know that genuine reality should include smudged and scabrous children, muddy roads on drizzly days, and, at least, sheep manure and dog-turds on country

102

greenswards. Of nineteenth-century American trash-piles and litter we know nothing for sure from pictures, but the general absence of ornamental yards in the homelier of Currier and Ives domestic views and in the house-plan books, too, would suggest a practical and bare environment for the mid-nineteenth-century American middle-class home. Kitchen gardens, of course, with neat rows and borders of ornamental herbs such as derive from medieval practice, are to be presumed, as are fences to keep out maurauding swine and ruminants.

The grander domestic scenes of Currier and Ives show the influence of Andrew Jackson Downing, and this brings us to the aristocratic English influence on the American home garden. In two words, the dominant contribution of the English to garden art is the picturesque landscape. These two words are not accidentally related to paint-ing; they were consciously taken from the two-dimensional arts of canvas and copper-plate and applied directly to the natural sur-roundings. Joseph Addison, writing in The Tatler and the Spectator was, early in the eighteenth-century, one of the first tastemakers to eschew the baroque geometry of the French and Italian Renaissance gardens. For the tone of the English new-found delight in picturesque nature, though, one can hardly do better than to quote the Earl of Shaftesbury (from Characteristicks): "I shall no longer resist the Pas-sion growing in me for things of a natural kind; where neither Art, nor the Conceit or Caprice of Man has spoiled that genuine Order, by breaking in upon that primitive State. Even the rude Rocks, the mossy Caverns, the irregular unwrought Grotto's, and broken Falls of Water, with all the horrid Graces of the Wilderness it-self as representing NATURE more, will be more engaging, and appear with a Magnificence beyond the formal Mockery of Princely Gardens." Of England's discovery of nature, Fletcher Steele rather dryly remarks that their "nature was already tamed scenery" and, as Elizabeth Wheeler Manwaring demonstrated in an exhaustive study of Italian Landscape in Eighteenth Century England, many of the English tech-niques were renderings of un-English paintings by Claude le Lorraine, Anthonie Waterloo, Salvator Rosa and others, where the wilds are attractively arranged about profound ruins, dancing nymphs and un-natural satyrs.

As pictures are framed, so the English park was framed, with vistas controlled by "naturally" spaced trees that afforded picturesque

glimpses of fields, forests, ruins, or cottages beyond - framed for the
appreciative eye and fringed by natural greenery, but umimpeded by
artificial walls and fences, whose practical office was disguised in
the ha-ha, or submerged wall. These techniques of framing out un-
picturesque peripheries from the field of vision and of using ha-ha
walls to disguise agricultural barriers were mainstays of A. J. Downing's landscaping. "The grand object in all this," he wrote, "should
be to open to the eye, from the windows or front of the house, a wide
surface, partially broken up and divided by groups and masses of trees
into a number of pleasing lawns or opening, differing in size and
appearance, and producing a charming variety in the scene. . . ."
This is the picturesque in Downing, as distinguished from the beautiful
(i.e., artificial) garden.

Irregularity is the key to Nature and the Picturesque. Indeed, William
Shenstone, who was, along with the less literary but more influential
"Capability" Brown ("this plot has capability for improvement," he
would tell delighted patrons), a major designer of English park-gardens,
wrote a poem on "the waving line."

> "Such is the waving line," they cry,
> "For ever dear to Fancy's eye!"
> Yon stream that wanders down the dale,
> The spiral wood, the winding vale,
> The path, which wrought with hidden skill,
> Slow twining scales yon distant hill
> With fir invested - all combine
> To recommend the waving line.
> The wreathed rod of Bacchus fair,
> The ringlets of Apollo's hair,
> The wood of Maia's offspring born,
> The smooth volutes of Ammon's horn.
> The structure of the Cyprian dome,
> And each fair female's beauteous frame
> Show to the pupils of Design
> The triumphs of the Waving Line.

To which ideal the satirist Richard Graves responded:

> Yet let not us inferior folks

> Expose ourselves to great men's jokes,
> But usefully our ground dispose,
> By planting cabbages in rows.

Partisanship in garden architecture surfaces from time to time, but never before or since has it equalled the contests of eighteenth-century England. Nonetheless, the quarrel between the views of Shenstone and Graves – indeed, the arguments that they employ – are eloquently representative of the differences between the cultivated and the popular traditions in America. For the former, Design is paramount; for the latter, usefulness. For the former, Fancy; for the latter, cabbages. For the former (tutored by Shenstone, Brown, Walpole, Rosa and Andrew Jackson Downing), the Waving Line; for the latter (in a tradition emphasized by "straight-plowing" contests in midwestern states), rows.

Andrew Jackson Downing was the translator and, to a degree, the democratizer, of the English picturesque garden-park for America, but in truth, his influence put more of a mark on democratic parks than on democratic gardens. I should not want to oversimplify our class structure, but in one respect the aristocracy of America is the collective, and its aristocratic parks of the Waving Line are public grounds. Frederick Law Olmstead and Calvert Vaux directly expressed Downing's views in New York City's Central Park, and the Downing-English tradition continues in such other parks as Philadelphia's Fairmont Park, Minneapolis-St. Paul's Mississippi Parkways, Chicago's Lincoln Park, and even to some extent in the federal Interstate Highway System.

Possibly a key to the difference between the Downing-style democratic park and the popular democratic garden is to be found in Downing's point of view in the quotation above – "from the windows or the front of the house." This is truly a perspective, as ego-centric as all the arts that we derive from the Renaissance. Nature was to be patterned to please the eye of man, from the perspective that please the comfort of man. The popular democratic garden, on the other hand, seems to be designed to please the visitor and the passerby quite as much as the resident. It seems to be a natural extension of the American state of mind that opens one yard to another in villages and cities, and opens lawns in the country right up to the road or highway. To preserve

this openness (which is a communal viewpoint) the popular tendency
was to keep the yard bare in the nineteenth century, and to cluster
shrubs and perennials around the house foundation in the twentieth
century. Both practices are repellent to landscape architects and to
designers. Yet they are as ubiquitous as the door-yard lilacs, which
decorate the house rather than screen it, and the plate glass "cottage
window" of the 1920's which became the "picture window" of the
1950's, both of which invited a view in rather than a vista out.

The people of America are incorrigible about their democratic yards.
The "picture window" was developed and named by designers whose
purpose was a modern version of the ideals of Shenstone and Capability Brown: to frame a controlled vista (in this case a backyard or
a distant horizon) for the picturesque pleasure of the home owner.
It was a living landscape to be part of the wall in the same manner
that an artist's landscape could be hung on a wall. Plate glass made
the picture-window a possibility not open to Shenstone and Downing –
and how they would have loved it! – but the unsophisticated people
of America perversely took the glass and incorporated it into the
democratic yard, where the house is the picture, not the yard. The
window, with evergreen bushes beneath it, is often decorated with a
lamp centered inside, or a large picture, mirror or whatnot shelf hung
on the opposite wall so that the passerby can be treated to a doubly
picturesque scene: the house and its plantings, the window and its
contents. What the insider sees, peering around the lampshade, is
the passerby.

There are exceptions, of course, not only in designer-planned yards,
but in those of many design-conscious persons. Education into the
cultivated traditions always alters or halts popular traditions, but the
statistical predominance of the democratic garden, open into a public
arena, ornamented to be picturesque for the outside, can be observed
by driving through any city, suburb, or farmland in America. The
power of this attitude toward yard and residence was strongly demonstrated to me recently in England. Driving through the Shropshire
hills, I suddenly came upon a ranch-style, hip-roofed, picture win-
dowed, open-yarded, shrubbed-foundationed house, with a naturally
forested slope behind, and the country-side was immediately, and
totally, deAnglicized, and the landscape became indistinguishable
from the Minnesota River valley around Mankato, where the nineteenth-

century Indian Wars had their start.

The picturesque garden for outside viewing has another ramification.
This is the use of ornaments (not ornamental plantings) on the lawn
and in the gardens. As often as not, these are displayed with a public orientation, that is, as a decorative focal point for the passing
cars. Once again, this is a popular phenomenon, not a cultivated
or aristocratic or even a civic practice; and, once again, its antecedents are elusive.

The ornaments are of three kinds that should be familiar to all Americans. The first of these three kinds derives from cultivated traditions and is mass-produced and mass-distributed for a fairly limited
trade. These include concrete, metal, ceramic and plastic reproductions of classical, Renaissance and oriental statuary: putti, urns,
gazing balls and stone-lanterns are three common examples. The
second kind is also manufactured, but the motifs are more modern,
and strangely enough, seem to derive more from folk traditions. These
include such things as plastic ducks and ducklings for the lawn, "Mexican" donkeys-and-carts, sleek Virgin Marys, fiberglass fountains,
ceramic frogs and such things. Verisimilitude and cute sentiment or
humor are characteristic of the second kind of ornament. The third
kind of ornament is most varied, original and interesting. These
decorations are homemade, frequently of cast-off materials. Birdhouses, miniature windmills, animals, nursery-rhyme figures, religious grottoes and "planters" of all kinds are variously made of wood,
spring metal, tin cans, bleach bottles, tires, bathtubs, beerkegs
and toilets. Related to these ornaments of all three kinds are decorative (and sometimes practical) fences. For popular gardens, however,
the fences rarely are substantial, and seldom express the firm privacy
of English and continental walls and hedges. Even in fences, the
American popular garden turns outward for the pleasure of the passing
parade. Thus, for example, the plastic reproductions of wrought iron
fences are often made with only one good side: this is to face outward.

Were we to grace these decorations with a cultivated past, we should
identify them with the "poetic" gardens of the always seminal eighteenth-century. Derek Clifford identifies some four garden-types that
developed in England during the time that the formal "architectural"

garden went through a transition into the "natural" park (but it should be remembered that these are not do-it-yourself democratic yards). One type, of course, was the picturesque, imitating Claude, Poussain and other landscapists. Another was the abstract, with neither architectural nor imitative content. The ferme ornée – the ornamented farm – was of the type that set Marie Antoinette playing at milkmaid. And the poetic garden was an illustration of some literary concept, depending upon statuary and interpretation of some kinds of associations, a "revival of the ancient worship of genius of place." The poetic garden is the precursor of Disneyland, tunnels of love and suchlike carnival reconstructions. One eighteenth-century English gentleman hired a hermit for his "savage garden," for example, and Sir William Chamber, in his Dissertation of Oriental Gardening (1772) proposed "electric shocks, artificial rain, contrived winds and explosions, and carefully planned earthquakes," as well as "beauteous Tartarean damsels in loose transparent robes, that flutter in the scented air, to present the master of the garden with rich wines, or invigorating infusions of Gingseng and amber. . . ."

These charming follies required a supportive industry of ornament manufacture. Paul Edwards, in English Garden Ornament seems to list lead sculpture, imported from the Low Countries, as the first of these mass-produced ornaments. In the nineteenth-century this was replaced by cast iron, "the material that helped to build the Industrial Revolution. . . . By the Great Exhibition of 1851, the Coalbrook Dale Company exhibited a most comprehensive range of cast iron and sometimes bronzed garden ornaments, which included ornamental park entrance gates, rustic domes, fountains, vases with cast iron bases, ornamental flower-pots, a serpent-handled vase and base for taking earthen flower pots, rustic ornamental seats, tables, flower stands and boot-scrapers." With the advent of mass-replicated ornaments, advertisements and catalogs from which both dealers and individuals might order, the garden was well on its way toward democratization.

Toward bastardization as well, for typically and predictably, the newcomer to a degree of wealth, property, and social aspiration tended to imitate the material trappings without suitably scaling down to the proportions of his land holdings. The iron deer that produced a sylvan effect when viewed from the house across a park-

land would, when planted in a front yard, produce the effect of iron deer only; the classical busts of stucco that produced the effect of an urbane Renaissance garden when spaced widely along a descending lawn would, when placed in a backyard adjoining a neighbor's lot, produce the effect of discordant imitation; the gazebo that produced a focal point for the eye and a resting place for the limbs in the environs of a stately mansion, would, when cramped a stone's throw from the porch of a Victorian city dwelling, produce the effect of an ostentatious outhouse.

In this century, with the further distribution of wealth and landscape, and with the development of even cheaper reproductions, to be disbursed more readily and more widely by means of rapid transportation, mail-order houses, franchised hardware stores and garden shops, the commercial progeny of the poetic garden and the ferme orneé, placed now on half-acre lots with hip-roofed "ramblers" become little Disneylands. The phenomenon is not American only: Paul Edwards, lamenting the suburban yards of England, said, in 1965, "Much of the decoration and ornament made for these gardens is part of the popular art of our times. Gnomes and dwarfs; concrete toadstools painted with white spots on a lurid red background; shoddy and ridiculously out-of-scale imitation well-heads, and concrete stoddle-stones [i.e., fieldstone or rusticated dressed-stone foundations] have been manufactured by the thousands, and used to make countless front gardens ridiculous. The essential ingredient of these ornaments is sentiment - everything else is sacrificed to this notion. To this end they must therefore imitate something familiar from the past, no matter how useless this object may now be or how unsympathetic this may be to the modern material being used." Edwards' irritability is modified only by the rather wistful hope that suburban ornament is "still a young art," and that improved techniques with ciment-fondu will permit higher standards.

In America, at least, there are some signs of relief from the lurid sentiment. Throughout the heyday of the cheap commerical ornament - the decade approximately 1955-1965 - there was little to choose from beyond the rather embarrassingly racist black stable boys and sombreroed sleepy peons, the flamingoes, ducks, and frogs, the strawhatted little fishermen, the sweet Morton's Salt girls, with umbrellas and Boston bulldogs, and sundry urinating types, clothed

or unclothed. The motifs, as we will see, were indeed drawn from "popular art of our times." But in recent years there have been more commonly available better-formed and better-cast ornaments - traditional and exotic, it is true, being often drawn from Japanese, Chinese, Hindu, Mayan and classical patterns - but nonetheless neither saccharine nor ludicrous. How these are utilized in the yard is a separate matter, and a greater test of taste and artistry, but it should be heartening to see inexpensive quality works available.

Possibly, though, the greatest translation of aristocratic garden art into popular art was augmented in the late Sixties by the development of cheap self-circulating electric pumps and extremely sturdy synthetic molding materials. Overall, the quality is depressingly artificial, with phoney boulders and White Rock Psyches, langorously drooping their nippleless breasts over a rainbow-lighted spray in the corner of the living room or beside the backyard swimming pool. The potential for everyman's being a king is there, though.

These were introduced in the 1969 Sears Roebuck Spring-Summer catalog thus:

A real show piece - inspired by the famous, lighted fountains of Rome, Paris, New York and Chicago. Entirely portable. . . .

Magnificently co-ordinated corner fountains with matching planters, plus foliage and tree. . . . So enchanting, so lovely. Every detail looks created by an interior decorator. . . . Made of marvelous Ceralon, ceramic polyvinyl chloride that's chip resistant. . . . No plumbing needed. ($9 per month) $99.99.

The foliage and the tree, of course, are also plastic, and the portability is representative of the peculiarly American sort of elegance that the same catalog carries for the first time to what may have been the ultimate in the democratic landscape. This is "Instant Shrubbery."

Lets you forget pruning, fertilizing, watering!
This shrubbery is made of magnificent polyvinyl chloride. Drought, disease, bugs don't bother it one bit. Stays spring green all year - untouched by windburn, freezeout or backbreaker snows that plague ordinary plantings. Perfect for new homeowners, architects,

builders. . . makes "just built" houses look handsomely finished.

And of the polyvinyl chloride Scotch pines:

> These man-made evergreens offer everything wished for in a
> live tree, and more! Each is magnificently shaped, lovelier
> even than nature.

A garden, Derek Clifford states, is "man's idealized view of the
world." This Sears Roebuck ideal may be that for the American popular garden, like it or not. Popular culture is outlaw culture, and no
responsible garden-lover can read the above without the feeling that
some crime has been committed, but for a society that has for two
centuries been committed to movement, to one-family residences, to
egalitarianism, to combat with wilderness and to the U. S. Patent
Office, plastic portable pines may be the highest expression of the
ideal.

There are aesthetic ideals implied in these ersatz evergreens, too,
for these are "foundation plantings," which are, for the popular
American home, just about as far as horticultural decoration is likely
to go. Even in nursery catalogs, where the evergreens are not of
polyvinyl chloride, the advertising appeal employs the same "instant
beauty" and real-estate approach. In the catalog of one of the
largest of these, Spring Hill Nurseries of Tipp City, Ohio, we can
read, for example, of a "Popular Taxus 'Picture Window' Sale."

> Quality assortment of America's finest evergreens quickly in-
> crease the beauty and value of your home. Ideal for foundation
> planting to enhance a picture window, the patio or the entrance.
> Aristocratic, trouble-free Taxus thrive in sun or shade, never
> outgrow their bounds and are free of pests and diseases. . . .

and immediately below, this offer:

> Top Quality do-it-yourself large, strong, rooted landscape size
> beautification group adds instant beauty to entrances, porches,
> picture windows, patios, etc. . . . .

III

There are a number of value expressions in these descriptions. First
of all, the reduction of beauty to formula is a garden variety of Edgar
Allen Poe's "Philosophy of Composition." Second, the promise that
these foundation plantings will "never outgrow their bounds" is an
assurance that the popular American penchant for clearing land will
not be violated. Third, the placement of plants under the picture-
window rather than within the prospect commanded by the view from
the house illustrates the reversal of the point of view of the English
aristocratic garden to that of the American democratic garden. Fourth,
the instant increase in value is an expression of the capitalistic rationale for beauty that is necessary to the American middle-class male.

All four of these interpretive points relate to one important fact which
may be surprising to many Americans, even when they are surrounded
by supporting evidence. This fact is that the popular ornamental home
garden is a very recent phenomenon in America, and its existence
even today may be a minority existence. In support of this statement,
let us first understand where the majority of Americans do not live.
They do not live in large houses on plots of a half-dozen acres or
more. They do not live in vine-covered cottages nor in Currier and
Ives farm houses.

Where they do live is in one-story real-estate development homes of
the Sixties, in duplex apartments of the Fifties, in two-bedroom Dutch
colonials and Cape Cods of the Thirties, in two-story flats and one-
story bungalows of the Twenties, in tenements of the 'Teens and in
high-rises and mobile homes of the Seventies, all on rectangular lots
that exploit every square foot of real-estate that zoning regulations
will permit. These are the majority democratic homes of America.
In rural areas as well, the majority of homes are small wooden houses –
some are shacks – or rectangular ramblers out of the same plan books
that give us the Levittowns of the suburban developments. Therefore,
when we look for the democratic garden, let us be certain that we
do not look into Better Homes and Gardens, Architectural Record,
Sunset or even Woman's Day where American yards and gardens put
their best feet forward. It is all too easy to drive along American
highways and see only the old handsome farmhouse, surrounded by
trees and outbuildings, far off, and ignore the mobile home park in
the foreground where one hundred times as many democrats live on
an equal-sized plot of ground.

I say this by way of definition, not as an indictment. There is a tendency, however, among students of popular culture sometimes to aim too high, not because of snobbery, I'm sure, but because the popular arts keep a low profile and are seen as a generalized mass, not as a collection of stereotyped individuals. Within each of those mobile homes lives a family, a group of people who make individual aesthetic choices according to group-sanctioned formulas, explicit or implicit. A vast network of competing industries are bolstering both the individuality and the stereotypes. A paradox, it is true, but it is the essential paradox of American popular culture.

But to return to ornamental gardens. It should be borne in mind that there is nothing about the homes of the majority of Americans that prevents gardening. Gardening is a matter of choice, not space. Nevertheless, many American homes have no gardens at all, more have a few foundation plantings, and relatively few have luxuriant gardens, designed for viewing from within or for strolling in. One reason for this, of course, is determined by limitations of money and time, and of the two, time is probably the greater factor. Hence, retired persons are more likely to ornament their homes. But the overwhelming reasons are traditional.

In 1932, Walter Prichard Eaton wrote an attractive little book called Everybody's Garden: Talks on Natural Design and the Use of Simple Material that expressed one aspect of the American anti-gardening tradition. In a chapter entitled "Men Wanted!," Eaton wrote, "The American husband is pretty good at pushing a lawn-mower (and altogether too good at raking the lawn. . .). But lawns are one of the social obligations, like paint on the house. A garden isn't a social obligation. It is an aesthetic frill, like writing poetry or putting pantalettes on lamb chops, both of which are beyond comprehension of most males." But until men do start gardening, Eaton maintained, "it will be difficult for a garden style to emerge in America which has masculinity and boldness, and which is not too much a matter of flower-beds, and not enough loving conformity to the native landscape and even the local flora."

These last two prescriptions for the use of the native landscape and the local flora are the predominant - indeed the almost exclusive - themes of American landscape artists, from Downing, through

113

Olmstead, to Jens Jensen, who developed much of the Chicago Park system early in this century - in some areas recreating the native Illinois wilds - and on to the present time. It is romantic, transcendental, Thoreavian. Even, as Eaton would have it, masculine; one might call it a mythic reenactment of the pioneer beginnings. But it is the wrong side of the myth, except to those rather subtle intellectuals who can discern design in natural forms, people who take pleasures in Whitman's free verse because of the design patterns of spoken English that it celebrates. In short, whereas all promoters of the American garden landscape urge native naturalism in their art, all the popular gardens insist upon artificiality, for, to the popular mind how can there be Art where one does not see the artifice?

Far more sympathetic to the popular mind and its formula aesthetic is a book by Edward W. Olver, Landscaping the Small Home, published in 1931, just a year before Eaton's Everybody's Garden. Olver says in his preface that it is a misconception that the average city or suburban lot from forty to seventy-five feet wide does not require any plantings. This is not the case, he continues, because "You purchased your home with the feeling that . . . it was well worth the actual cash investment required. Naturally, in planning to beautify the front or public part of the grounds, the main consideration must be to make the house the center of the picture. All plantings made in the front area must serve the purpose of accentuating the particular attractions of the house, rather than drawing interest away from it. Thus it is not good taste to hide the view from the street, or to plant showy or exotic trees or shrubs in that area." The italics I have supplied to emphasize the contrast with Eaton's cynicism about "social obligations" and his romantic ideas about "natural design." The popular American home is a public statement of pride of ownership, and to the democratic mind obligation is to social harmony, not to natural harmony. We did not conquer the wilderness just to give it back, but to make a place for our own homes. It would indeed be poor taste to hide this community achievement. The balance of Landscaping the Small Home is made up of formulae based on this practical rationale. For example, the entrance is the focal point of the house, so "Either side of the entrance should be accented by plants graceful in form, and somewhat larger than those used in other parts of the planting, with smaller, dwarf growing plants in front and beside them," while "The remainder of the foundation planting is selected to harmonize

114

with entrance planting, to give outline to the bed and to cover the house foundation, if it is unattractive."

One year prior to this, another book had also been entitled Everybody's Garden, this one written by Frank A. Waugh. Waugh finds himself caught between the two camps, and really does much toward summarizing for us the dichotomies and paradoxes of American popular garden landscaping. First, he does allow that much has been justly said about how American families neglect their gardens, and do not live within them as do the English. The English garden is inspired by "the spirit of privacy." "Why," says Waugh, "the privacy of English gardens is so great as to make them favorite courting grounds and meeting places of engaged couples. In this country a young man would as soon meet his girl in front of the department store show window as in the garden. . . ." Yet the American idea has merits. "I am glad," he continues, "that it is neither necessary nor fashionable for all my neighbors to shut themselves and their gardens up in high brick walls. The more especially as regards their good American front yards. . . . Even the fences between different lots are gone down, and there is nothing left to show the line between Mr. Higbee's lawn and Mr. Meredith's. This is nothing more nor less than a fine, free, physical expression of the American idea of equality. It is the spirit of democracy." The remainder of Waugh's Everybody's Garden tries to balance the two, allowing for public democracy in the front yard and private intimacy in the back. He is, though, aware that this cannot be achieved on too small a plot of ground and his answer begs the question: it simply insists that American yards should be bigger to accommodate "the broad effects and the spacious freedom of this optimistic American feeling."

Waugh also laments the prevailing femininity of American gardens. "As a landscape architect with a moderate professional experience I have learned to beware of a blue-eyed, golden-haired woman under 40 who emphasizes the information that she is 'passionately fond of flowers.'" By and large, American landscape architects have not been florists - or women. And, the excesses of femininity in gardening have sometimes been a bit hard to stomach. For instance, Alice Morse Earle's Old-Time Gardens, A Book of Sweet O' the Year (published in 1901, reissued in 1928) speaks of the "Ladies' Delight" blossom thus: ". . . it is such a shrewd, intelligent little creature

that it readily found out that spring was here ere man or other flowers knew it. This dear little primitive . . . has a score of folk names, all testifying to an affectionate intimacy: Bird's-eye; Garden-gate; Johnny-jump-up; None-so-pretty; Kitty-come; Kit-run-about; Three-faces-under-a-hood; Come-and-cuddle-me; Pink-of-my-Joan; Kiss-me; Tickle-my-fancy; Kiss-me-ere-I-rise; Jump-up-and-kiss-me." Mrs. Earle's style, however, disguises a fine amateur scholar, for she is an excellent historian of garden art. Her chapter on "Tussy-Mussies," for instance, is based on a masculine term from 1629, with a considerable etymological dissertation on the work; all of her folk-names are valuable dialect collections.

As a matter of fact, women came very late to garden art – they were characteristically weeders, and nothing more. We can almost date the entrance of English and American women into gardening with certainty, and when they do come in, it is with authority rather than sentiment. In Britain, Jane Loudon, wife of the encyclopedist-gardener John Loudon, wrote Gardening for Ladies in the early 1840's. Hers is no simpering gentility: she is speaking of digging, wheel-barrowing, manuring and fighting slugs. In America, we can probably date women's involvement in gardening from 1869, with Catherine Beecher and Harriet Beecher Stowe's compendium of domestic science, The American Woman's Home. The Beecher sisters' decorative gardening is limited to house plants, however.

But their highly influential book relates to the overall subject of the democratic garden in another sense, for they direct the problem of beautifying the home toward a very low economic group, far below Downing's clients and even below the middle-class owners of the fifty-foot lots of the 1930s. The popular democratic garden at the lower end of the economic scale must be decorated with resource-fulness. Let us quote the Beechers at length:

"Just here, perhaps, we are met by some who grant all that we say on the subject of decoration by works of art, and who impatiently exclaim, 'But I have no money to spare for any thing of this sort. I am con-demned to an absolute bareness, and beauty in my case is not to be thought of.'

"Are you sure, my friend? If you live in the country, or can get

116

into the country, and have your eyes opened and your wits about you, your house need not be condemned to absolute bareness. Not so long as the woods are full of beautiful ferns and mosses, while every swamp shakes and nods with tremulous grasses, need you feel yourself an utterly disinherited child of nature, and deprived of its artistic use.

"For example: Take an old tin pan condemned to the retired list by reason of holes in the bottom, get twenty-five cents worth of green paint for this and other purposes, and paint it. The holes in the bottom are a recommendation for its new service. If there were no holes, you must drill two or three, as drainage is essen.- tial. . . ." This becomes a hanging basket for ferns and grasses. "On the same principle you can convert a salt-box or an old drum of figs into a hanging-basket." Another wall planter is made of an old "ox-muzzle" nailed onto a decorative board. In these passages we are shown the beginning of a folk-popular art, one based on home ownership, do-it-yourself manuals, creative resourcefulness -- and junk. In a rural paper that Harriet Beecher Stowe edited, the Hearth and Home, children were trained into the creative use of junk on "Our Boys and Girls Page." Lament- ing the fact that land-clearing and hunting had driven away birds from the American yard, on March 1, 1873, C. C. Haskins gave the following tips on "Simple Birdhouses:"

". . . Save or get oyster-kegs - the large size - and wash them thoroughly. . . ." "Now, if you have ingenuity enough to make a nice martin-box . . . get a couple of boxes, like candle or soap boxes. . ." "You little folks who cannot make a box for birds, go up in the garret and get an old hat, tear out the lining, cut a hole about an inch in diameter in the top, and nail the outer rim to the edge of the house." Three weeks following, Hearth and Home was advocating "adult" bird houses made from bark and other natural materials. In 1879, another home economist, Mrs. Julia McNair Wright, in The Complete Home provided the following recipes for using junk for garden beauty: "no old barrel-hoops rotted on the ground there: they were used for fences to the garden bed, and for frames for vines." Immigrants, too, were indoctrinated into using cast-off materials, and along with that, in the aesthetic of the

117

American yard. C. P. Dwyer's The Immigrant Builder or Practical Hints to Handy-Men, (tenth edition, 1878) states that "It is always advisable to build a house back from the road at least sixty feet, so as to admit of a front plot or flower-garden. Some build on, or close to the roadside; but this is not at all desirable, as pigs, poultry, &c., will make it a hard matter to keep the front of the house anything like clean; and the fragrant beauty of the flower-garden is worth all the pains and trouble that may be bestowed on it. A cottage home with a neat exterior is like a well-dressed person; it draws attention to it-self, and the possessor is justly proud of it." The architectural context for these statements, incidentally, is sod, adobe and rammed-earth houses with earth floors hardened with cow's-blood, and the furniture is "the barrel-chair," candle box foot-stools, and mattresses filled with cattails. Dwyer calls these "makeshifts which necessity suggests," but he goes on to say, "No matter how small the dwelling, or how humble the beginning of the pioneer, there are a great many little ways in which he can add real luxuries to his homestead," such as "rustic seats out-of-doors for summer-evening enjoyment."

In other words, the homely ornaments of the American popular garden were born with the Homestead Act. Independent ownership of land, no matter how freely purchased, is a ticket to leisure of the yard, and this leisure can be beautified with materials at hand: ox-muzzles, leaky pans, flour barrels and barrel-hoops, swamp-grasses and unpeeled branches. This, though, is outlaw art, and by 1914, George W. Cable, novelist and social critic of the New South, was complaining of "toy gardens," with "cerulean sewer-pipe crested with scarlet geraniums, rows of whited cobbles along the walk or drive like a cannibal's skulls around his hut, purple paint-kegs of petunias on the scanty door-steps, crimson wash-kettles of verbenas, ant-hill rockeries, and well-sweeps and curbs where no wells are. . . ." Almost twenty years later, Walter Prichard Eaton devoted a whole vituperative chapter to such "doodads," even though he rather admired the forthright use of broken bottles as a geometric design in one garden: "I thought it was terrible, but the owner liked it very much, and as she was a product of an artificial society, it fitter her style nicely."

Such a degree of aesthetic charitableness is rare. Ordinarily aesthetic gardeners do not deign to see the doodads made of junk, but those who do consign them to the antiparadise in a sentence or two. But Eaton's

recognition of the artificial mind of the popular garden artist is
rarer yet. Some popular minds can read books in brooks and sermons
in stones, but for most, art and culture must be artificial. The mid-
dle-ground of Whitman's verse, of Jensen's reconstructed prairie
river, of Downing's ha—has, of Shenstone's Waving Line, are, to
the popular mind, not nearly so artistic as rhymes of Poe's, and cabbages in rows.

There is a startling originality to folk-popular garden art. Red, white
and blue fence posts capped variously with plastic cast-off bottles
from Wisk, Clorox and All, as I have seen in Missouri; toilets with
geraniums blazing from snowy bowls in Wisconsin and Minnesota;
up-ended bathtubs making shell-like grottoes for plaster Virgins in
Colorado; planters of disemboweled hot-water tanks from coast-to-
coast and border-to-border, and tires! Tires for fences, hedges,
planters, bumpers, swings. Bleach bottles for birdhouses, bird-feeders,
wind-toys, outdoor Christmas decorations. Mailboxes of welded
chains, pumps, sewing machine stands, milk cans, beer barrels - and
never of colors to hint at nature, sentiment or romance. They are
all pure artifice -- "the popular art of our times," as the English
chronicler of outdoor ornament, Paul Edwards named them.

But all is not this joyous reclamation of litter. There is also the
popular outgrowth of the "poetic garden:" garden sticks. These,
sticks with jigsawed and enameled images of birds, Miss Muffets,
and cartoon characters, were a phenomenon of the Thirties; partly,
I suppose, fostered by the enforced leisure of unemployment; but
also fostered by Industrial Arts in the schools: Lovell and Hall's
1937-1942 Index to Handicrafts, Modelmaking and Workshop Projects
lists sixteen recipes for garden sticks in addition to 103 garden ornaments - plus various arbors, birdhouses, trellises, weathervanes and
windmill models - many of the indexed references being to patterns
in industrial education magazines. It is reasonable to assume that
many of the ornaments came from school woodworking shops, but in
addition to that source for the patterns, such magazines as Popular
Mechanics and Popular Science served as national clearing houses
for ideas and patterns, including such handyman oddities as a 1950
garden vase made entirely of bottle-caps. This tradition, however,
probably originates with Hearth and Home in the years following the
Civil War.

119

These patterns dissolve into "patio furniture" in the Fifties, and by 1955, the homemade projects are supplanted by commercial plastic garden sticks such as Sears Roebuck sold. The folk-popular motifs virtually disappear by 1970, when the elegance of Renaissance poly-vinyl chloride fountains puts Miss Muffet to shame. Two other upcult influences are observable by the late Sixties, one being the ecology-inspired idea of re-cycling junk, the other the pop-art inspired idea of "found art," as in an attractive idea-book entitled New Uses for Old Cannonballs, written by David Van Dommelen, and in the 1974 show mounted by the Walker Art Center of Minneapolis that gathered from coast-to-coast the best and most monumental examples of popu-lar junk art. And with that legitimization of junk, we may bring this chapter to a close.

But for such a long and complicated chapter, a summary seems ad-visable. As the foregoing paragraph indicates, the democratic gar-den is a dynamic art, and any summary must be regarded as being in transit. Still, some four broad conclusions are possible. First, there is no direct tradition for the American popular garden that reaches back much earlier than the middle of the nineteenth century. Gar-dens for the well-to-do - which are not relevant to this study - are ordinarily scaled-down reflections of the predominate European styles. Public gardens in America include some of the baroque for-mal tradition, but these are not part of a continuous tradition; rather, like Williamsburg, they are reconstructions. The typical cultivated American public garden is of eighteenth-century English origin, by way of Downing, Olmstead and Jensen. Even the picnic areas of National Parks and National Forests follow this tradition of waving lines, nature tamed, and framed vistas.

Secondly, the popular democratic garden appears to be based on the clearing. Up to the present day, the tendency among American home owners has been to clear and grade the environs of their homes. Two technological developments following the Civil War augmented this practice. The lesser of these was barbed-wire which made it easier to fence out cattle, thereby permitting larger, more open yards. The greater innovation was the lawn mower, patented in 1869, which made it possible to mow a greensward without engaging special gardeners to handmow with a scythe.

A third conclusion is that in America, the house is not only the focal interest of the grounds, but that maintenance of the external appearance of house and grounds is a social and economic obligation rather than an individual pleasure. The ornament and design, therefore, are designed for public view and community consistency rather than for picturesque vistas from within the home.

Fourth, designs and patterns are perpetuated both by example as well as by popular publications. The popular garden is truly democratic in being a do-it-yourself project. Ornament, consequently, has been inexpensive and stereotyped, but has included extremely original use of junk material as artificial garden decoration. In most cases, however, these are lawn ornaments, and appear to be a folk-art form that may have originated out of necessity of beginnings, as Harriet Beecher Stowe and C. P. Dwyer seem to suggest, and yet they are to be found ornamenting secure, sedate and conventional popular homesteads in suburbs, towns and countryside throughout America. Sometimes they are to be found with the older home landscape tradition of lawn, separated flower garden, and shade tree, but without foundation planting, fence or hedge to restrict the view of the house; other times they will be ornamenting the newer pattern of open lawn and evergreen foundation plantings that are placed where the house is open to public view, as in picture window and entrance plantings. It should be pointed out that there is an upper middle class tradition that persists in neighborhoods of large houses built in the Twenties, wherein the front lawn is clear, major corner shrubberies frame the house, and the back yards are separated by heavy plantings of unpruned flowering shrubs. This relatively small enclosed private yard is a landscape-architect style originating in early twentieth-century Germany with Lichtwark's and Avenarius' Freilufthauser - open-air houses.

This style, and a post-World War II pool-and-patio tradition, are the crucial one social step up from the native American popular democratic garden, but they are dependent upon a relatively large plot of ground, a conscious awareness of design, and a degree of leisure that can regard the outdoors as a recreational extension of the living and dining areas. All three of these requisites - large lot, conscious design, and leisure - have an important prerequisite - money.

Those who have not such a resource must be resourceful, as <u>Farmer's Law</u> would indicate. And they will be resourceful, defining garden art as artifice, an ornament to the American home. Self-confident but unsubtle, their yards may offend the sensibilities of those who do not live in them, but such is the way of the popular aesthetic. It is outlaw, but of a rather heroic sort of rob-from-the-rich-give-to-the-poor sort. For that reason, I retain my faith in bleach bottles, broken glass and truck-tire swings. The people who display these flotsam of the twentieth-century are not to be bested by obsolescence or debris. They fit the cast-offs of prosperity to their quest for beauty. And the beauty which they achieve is as irrepressibly democratic and as flamboyantly cock-sure as the lilacs of spring.

Politics, Pratika and Plastic Jesus

God must have loved the popular artifact, because he made so many
of them.   This statement characterizes an easy trap to fall into,
particularly for those students of popular culture who love humanity,
and who are given to Jeffersonian faith in the common man. One
man's vote is as good as another's, and the democratic majority is
guide enough for our ships of state. Why then should not majority
taste be as sure a guide in aesthetics? The question is almost unan-
swerable, because it contains a network of assumptions that are ques-
tionable in themselves, such as the assumption that democratic majority vote really is the best political guide, or the assumption that
politics and arts are in any way comparable. However, the main fal-
lacy in the analogy between art and politics, and in the doctrine of
democratic sanction for determining what is "good" or even "best" in
either politics or the arts, is the assumption that the common man has
free and open choice in his selection. But unfortunately the common
man selects the "best" from a limited slate of familiar candidates,
not from an unlimited horizon of possibilities. Furthermore, the
common man's slate of candidates is preselected, tailored, manipulated
and promoted according to the preconceptions of a coterie of opinion-
makers and tastemakers who are attempting to anticipate the wishes of

the majority on the basis of the behavior of past majorities, and on the basis of the information that they are provided by other similar coteries.

This ravel of influences and processes in the arts is most readily understood by expanding on the political analogy. The democratic choice exercised in American presidential elections applies only to the final slate. Better men may have been eliminated during a nom-inating convention, better <u>women</u> may have been eliminated from consideration at the first mention of their names at a Washington cocktail party. Potential winners may have been dissuaded from candidacy in a year when their party presumes defeat. Dark horses are invented at a slight rotation of fortune's wheel. The majority find themselves voting for strangers as vice-presidential candidates. Opinion pollsters and advertising agencies assure the people of what is their will. Traditions in America reduce all choices to either Republican or Democrat. Virtually all knowledge of candidates that flows toward the voter has its source in the meetings of campaign managers and press agents, and is filtered through the prejudices, the time limitations, the deadlines and competitions of the media.

The same complexities apply to popularity in the arts. Popular recorded music, for example, is full of contrived dark horse candi-dates, vice-presidential flip-sides, and press-agential opinion polls. Similarly, drama gets to Broadway by paths nearly equivalent to the paths to Capitol Hill, while a painter can be elevated to popularity by the combination of a <u>Time</u> magazine review, an interview on the <u>Tonight</u> show, a cut-and-paste reproduction in <u>Woman's Day</u>, a couple Hallmark cards, and a January spot on an ecumenical religious calen-dar.

In other words, it is an oversimplification to accept popularity as the people's sanction of quality, or as embodying the expression of the popular mind. In the realm of <u>folk</u> culture, however, the romantic ideal of popularity as an expression of popular will, and popular will as a manifestation of the Good, is somewhat more valid than is the case in a mass culture. A tribal culture, a non-literate rural culture, leaves no one in the dark about politics or art. A Paraguayan Indian, selecting either a leader or an amulet, does not have his choice limited by the restrictions of remote, anonymous intermediaries; he

is given no slate of uncorporeal candidates. His choice is limited only by his horizons, and regardless of how provincial and "primitive" this may make him, his horizons are natural horizons, not artificial impositions. His decisions may be subject to manipulation, but the manipulators are before him in the day, and beside him as his neighbors throughout the nights.

It is all too easy for us to reduce this natural liberty to universal law, thereby making a virtue of narrow experience and parochial choice, and making a vice of teflon, Angel records and winter strawberries, all of which are blessings of mass culture and technology. But we cannot have both the winter strawberries and the natural liberty; no, sad to say, it is impossible for us to achieve cosmopolitan experience, boundless horizons and indefinite perfectibility without accepting mass production, technical proficiency and the media along with them.

But this is only a preface to the consideration of popular religious art. A preface is necessary because the serious consideration of popular religious art is impossible without accepting the dictum that God must have loved the popular artifact, because he made so many of them; and that dictum is childish without clear-headed qualification.

Because the fact of the matter is that the religious experience has no aesthetic restrictions. The glories of religious art are products of the religious experience, not prerequisites to it. The quality of religious experience that comes to a Roman Catholic from contemplation of a garish chromo of the sacred heart is not necessarily less than what he would derive from an original El Greco altar-painting. There is nothing to suggest that the experiences of Moses, Buddha, Jesus, Mohammed, Francis of Assisi, Martin Luther, Ralph Waldo Emerson, Mary Baker Eddy, Joseph Smith or Billy Graham were triggered by or derived from art works. Savonarola contributed toward Michelangelo's frescos, Luther toward Dürer's Praying Hands, but there seems to be no reciprocal influence. In spite of this apparent one-way thoroughfare from religion to art, almost every religion has generated more works of art than has any other cultural or social force, and, in addition to this, the popular audience has, throughout the ages, derived its primary inspiration -- and what is more important, its religious sustenance -- from art works. Thus, religious art of all

kinds is best regarded as popular art and as functional art. Indeed, the examination of religious art may do more toward differentiating between the popular tradition and the cultivated tradition, and between social functions and aesthetic functions of the arts than can the study of any other field of the arts.

In the usual senses, the study of popular arts cannot give consideration to arts prior to the industrial revolution, for mass production, mass society, and mass art go hand in hand. Before industrialization, the arts were almost entirely individual and were the products of either a conscious tradition of cultivated craftsmanship and self-expression, or of a folk tradition of unrationalized anonymous provincial expression.

The exception is religious art, and a big exception it is. Mass production of religious artifacts is a phenomenon common to all centuries, extending back to the Egyptians; and it is common to all civilizations, even into the Himalayan reaches of Asia. In Egypt, amulets and charms were produced from molds in sufficient abundance to make antique faience scarabs available today in museum shops at very low prices, and one may see at anthropological museums cases filled with the molds used in ancient Egypt and in Tibet for the mass production of identical religious figures for their mass religions. The necessity of mass religion is what puts limits on the geographic extent of mass production of religious art. Thus, the religious art of a folk culture is folk art, as in the case of many native African tribal religions. The common characteristics of African ancestral figures -- the recurrent "muntu" face, for example -- are common not in the same sense that all pressings of a Frank Sinatra record are identical, but they are common in the same sense that all versions of Barbara Allen share certain elements that show little change from artist to artist, from audience to audience. But even this is rather involved, for the repetitive patterns of Mexican retablos, regardless of how much they are folk art, iconologically conform to dogmatic standards; that is, while they are individually worked, not mass-produced, they are yet symbolic manifestations of a mass religion. In the early days of Christian Mexico, the patterns and symbols were unequivocally forced upon the native Santeros, or "saint-makers," because these images could become the visible, concrete extension of the arm of the church into each peon's hut. As time went on, however, there was a relaxation

of the regulations, but this was possible because the Santeros had the
episcopal force replaced by the parochial force, and finally, by the
easy sanctions of community tradition, the super-ego that tells the
local artist: "That is the way it has always been done; that is the way
it was done in the beginning; that is the way you will do it now."
This is the essence of folk religious art.

In folk art, the variations are more often the results of the slip of the
brush, a short-circuit in the memory, a narrowness of experience,
than they are the results of spiritual upheaval or wilful self-expression.
The artist who supplies a native flower in his picture of the crucifixion
is probably not saying "I will express my culture with this flower;" he
is probably simply painting the only flower he knows in the place in
the picture where a flower is required by tradition.

To return to popular mass-produced art. Religion in any complex
society operates as the primary positive cohesive force. There are
other bonds, of course: language, geography, history, but these are
not so readily described as forces in a dynamic sense; rather, they
are static associations. But there are other forces: government, the
military, bureaucracy: yet these are often highly negative forces,
that is, they act in opposition, or repression, or control of the people.
Furthermore, in most societies, government is a sometime thing; wherever it is constantly apparent, it is totalitarian and negative and
eventually becomes intolerable, but wherever it is infrequently apparent, government loses its authority, and while it is not negative,
it ceases to be cohesive. The problem in unifying a society, therefore, is one of keeping central control by being constantly apparent,
but in a positive way. Bread and circuses will do the job, and so
will fighting a common enemy, but both approaches are sinkholes for
the public weal, and cannot go on forever. It is not only the economic drain that causes these to be unsatisfactory cohesive forces,
for endless welfare debilitates and cloys and militant vigilance is
tiring and hazardous.

These remarks, however, are best kept general, for any historical
illustration is likely to precipitate moot deposits in any already misty
argument, but I propose that any historical instance of a complex
society that possesses cohesiveness must have a mass religion. Often
the mass religion is indistinguishable from patriotism, and thus provides

a cohesive force to sustain militarism; other times it borders on continuous festival, and thus provides a cohesive support for a welfare state; but in any case, religion (or quasi-religion) provides both uniformity and universality. The uniformity is easy enough to understand, and in a theatrical sense, it is an important part of popular culture: the mass rallies in Red Square, the mass audiences before St. Peter's, the ritual sacrifices at Tenochtitlan; these all bring men and women together into unified mass of one focal point, of one voice, of one will; but, to put a secular cast on the psychology of it all, "where should we go after the show?" At rallies, on feast days, on sabbath days, religion can presume that a mass audience will operate as the anonymous recipients of a consistent and unvarying ritual, but when the rally is over and the festival is past, the Sunday-night blues settle upon us; and then the mass religion needs sustenance. The sustenance must come by means of dispersing the religious experience among the homes and into the lives of the masses. Regardless of how easily human beings can be manipulated to surrender their egos into a mass experience, no one likes impersonality for very long. Mass religion must have a personal extension program, for eventually we must come home, and if it can be arranged that we come home to a ritual microcosm of the mass experience, our transcendent sabbath will be confirmed daily and thereby be sustained until the next sabbath rolls around.

What I say is not new; it was the consciously-wrought rationale for practical application in Nazi Germany. No German could sustain himself as a Nazi from rally to rally all by himself, but if he came home with a swastika on his arm to see his flag and his fuehrer on the mantel-piece, and to incorporate the "religion" into the simplest social exchange with a "Heil Hitler," the uniform belief could be sustained in microcosm until the next rally. It is not pleasant to think about, but it is most terribly important for everyone to remember Hitler's great experiment in applied popular culture, for the German experience is an example that should assure us of the urgency of our developing the ability to discriminate among popular arts between those things that are directed toward us as mass beings and those that serve us all with wider choices to suit our individual tastes.

But I do not wish to place undue emphasis on cynical quasi-religions

and manufactured religiosity in a consideration of popular religious art. Nevertheless, it will be seen that my earlier political analogy was neither accidental nor incidental; popularity in religion and politics may not always represent the popular mind. It may represent submission to autocratic will, or it may represent the most expedient choice from an undemocratically selected state of candidates. Thus, God <u>may</u> love the popular artifact, because there are so many of them, but it ain't necessarily so.

Notwithstanding, no state or tribal religious control can continue without a mass-sanctioned aesthetic; that is, as in all popular arts, the product must sell. It must anticipate needs, it must respond to unstructured criticisms of the constituency, it must flex with social-psychological changes that have been wrought by other forces -- economic, climatic, military, epidemiological -- but at the same time it must provide for individual, family and clan worship that is consistent and compatible with the politics and government of the day. It is in this respect that Jeffersonian faith in the will of the people is valid; no people will accept for long that which they do not like; or, to put it in a positive sense, popular culture has a life of its own that ignores daily events. When a popular art work really expresses the beliefs of the people and responds to their needs, it will resist all imposed changes, all higher criticism, and will achieve the outlaw immortality that all popular culture strives toward, not to be recognized until much later by upcult critics.

A particularly strong set of examples are to be found in the Roman Catholic sacred heart artifacts, and the "plastic Jesus" family of artifacts which are icons that affect even the most fundamentalist of Protestant sects. The sacred heart icon should be familiar to any denizen of the western world. In pictures and in statues it is to be found on all continents, most frequently in the mode of open-heart surgery on the Christ or the Blessed Virgin Mary, but oftentimes as a disembodied organ, entwined with roses and barbed wire. The pervasiveness of the sacred heart image suggests official sanction and promulgation; the ecstatic dignity of the holy figures suggests culti-vated antecedents by the great masters of the Renaissance, and yet neither of these is the case, for the cult of sacred heart did not start until the middle of the seventeenth century with St. John Eudes, its popularity being augmented by the mystical experience of St.

Margaret Mary Alacoque; while the earliest image of the sacred heart does not appear until 1780, in a painting by the very minor Italian artist, Pompeo Batoni. Further, insofar as the New Catholic Encyclopedia can be regarded as a trustworthy official voice, the church condemns the aesthetics of the cult in these irritable terms: "Statues and paintings of disputable taste, often of vulgar sentiment repulsive to educated sensibilities, proliferated from the beginning of the nineteenth century;" a time incidentally, that coincides with the development of the mechanical mass production of visual art objects.

The sacred heart iconography, therefore, is an ideal example of the independent existence of popular arts. The sacred heart, despite its repugnance in the eyes of cultivated beholders, clearly must fulfill important needs to the illiterate worshiper. Here is a case where the long-term and wide-spread proliferation of the images must be taken as popular sanction, not passive acceptance. In this case, God must have loved the popular icon because he made so many of them. Indeed, while the specific pictures may be distasteful to the church, the church policy in respect to religious images is based on the right of every communicant, literate or illiterate, to receive, properly interpreted, the word of God. So long as literacy is not a democratic right, the picture and the statue are necessary media of communication, and hence, the altarpiece, the stations, and the church windows have been media of mass communication, not mass-produced, it is true, but entirely as effective media for reaching a mass audience as electric bull-horns or sky-writing.

But when mass-produced popular media came upon the scene, the simple ideal ceased to be simple. With the invention of movable type printing around 1450, literacy became not only theoretically desirable, but practically useful. That is, just as learning to speak a foreign language is useless unless one has some one to speak to, so, learning to read had been useless before there were cheap books available for reading. With books being practically possible, the series of influences that lead to Luther and the Reformation only sixty years later is one of the most bewildering cases of headlong inevitability in all history, with all the branches of history in a pile-up on the exit ramp; technological, political, diplomatic, educational, military, intellectual, philological, social and religious

events all crowding out of the medieval mainstream at once.

Religious art was one of the first casualties. If literacy was practical, the arguments for visual art as necessary for mass communication lost their compelling validity, and iconography was open to attack as idolatry. These attacks could be fended, if somewhat belatedly, in the Council of Trent's 1563 decrees that "the images of Christ, of the Virgin Mother of God, and of the other saints are to be placed and retained especially in the churches, and that due honor and veneration is to be given them; not, however, that any divinity or virtue is believed to be in them by reason of which they are to be venerated, or that something is to be asked of them, or that trust is to be placed in images . . . but because the honor which is shown them is referred to the prototypes which they represent, so that by means of the images . . . we adore Christ and venerate the saints whose likeness they bear." Further, "no representation of false doctrines and such as might be the occasion of grave error to the uneducated may be exhibited . . . ," and "nothing may appear that is disorderly or unbecoming and confusedly arranged . . . ," above all, "no one is permitted to erect or cause to be erected in any place or church, howsoever exempt, any unusual image, unless it has been approved by the bishop. . . . "

This is all well and proper and it led to very close supervision of artists commissioned to the painting of church art, but it could not stay the flood of popular mass-produced art, because the same processes that made the printing press made the popular woodcut print possible. Prior to the Reformation, religious cuts of saints were produced in convents and sold at shrines; but there was no necessary corner on the production of those cuts in the monastic confines, and it was an easy extension of secular woodcarving and joinery into the mass production of religious pictures. Ironically enough, Luther's attacks on the church were directed at popular mass production of religious goods at the same time that his translation of the Bible and his ideal of "every man his own priest" were made possible by mass printing. The very crudeness of woodcuts of the fifteenth and sixteenth century points to a popular tradition devoid of formal aesthetic, particularly when one contrasts the works executed in the next mass art media to be developed, that of metal engraving and etching, which developed among goldsmiths, whose training was in art as

well as practical craftsmanship. It is, incidentally, worth noting that the earliest etchings were of playing cards. The media of popular culture are most effective in satisfying the requirements of standardization and repetition, both characteristics being necessary to honest card-playing -- and to cohesive, conforming and Catholic religion.

The historical pile-up circa 1500 has had profound repercussions on all of the arts. One of the most reverberant of the effects of mass production has been in the fixing of styles of 1500, most dramatically for us is the case of English spelling, for Caxton and others produced English Bibles and other books at a time when our language was changing with breathtaking speed. Thus, the pre-Caxton world of English literature from Caedmon through Chaucer and Skelton was able to communicate by phonetic spelling of the contemporary speech, but when a typesetter set the word knight, still largely phonetic in spelling, at the same time that the spoken tongue was evolving the word into nīt, the die was cast along with the type, and we have been left with a literary language only tangentially related to the spoken language. It is not the printers who are to blame; it is the mass distribution of printed matter that is to blame, for revising spelling is as hopelessly complicated in a mass society as is revising a system of weights and measures. Mass-produced popular culture standardizes artifacts and activities in every chimney-corner of civilization.

But it was not only language in England that was changing in this period of time, and there was more going on in Europe than religious reform. This was the Renaissance, and the changes in painting were more rapid and earlier than any of the other changes. From Gentile de Fabriano and Sasseta in the early Fifteenth century (circa 1430) to Raphael at the dawn of the new century, is for the common viewer as much of a shift from "ancient" and foreign to modern and familiar as is the shift from Chaucer to the King James Bible to the common reader, and both the King James Bible and Raphael pervade all Christian utterances to this day. It is Raphael's madonnas who stand back of nearly every popular sacred heart, pietá, or holy family, and where Raphael is obscured, other Renaissance hands are to be found: Leonardo, Mantegna, della Robbia, or somewhat later, Velazquez and Zurburan, but most often it is Raphael's sweet faces, his elevated depictions of motherhood, and his clearlighted, equipoised and

uncluttered compositions that are to be found simplified, provincialized
and sometimes bastardized in innumerable altarpieces, retablos,
shrines, calendars, Christmas cards, medals, bookmarks, presentation
Bibles, catechisms -- and in devout minds throughout the world.
Raphael by himself was a veritable madonna-factory, but his students
and imitators perpetrated his vision on parish altars, in hand-executed
copies and in popular engravings until lithography, chromolithography
and rotary printing could almost completely supplant the human agent
in popular religious art. The sweetness turned into sentiment, the
elevation turned into vacant formulae, and the clarity into flat noth-
ingness. All these characteristics are discernable in popular sacred
hearts, but they are legitimate progeny of Renaissance art.

Of Raphael's genius, Vasari wrote: "With the death of this admirable
artist painting might well have died also, for when he closed his eyes
she was left all but blind. We who remain can imitate the good and
perfect examples left by him, and keep his memory green for his genius and the debt which we owe to him. It is, indeed, due to him that
the arts, colouring and invention have all been brought to such perfection that further progress can hardly be expected, and it is unlikely
that anyone will ever surpass him."

The characteristics of Raphael that Vasari so much admired are just
those characteristics that distress Kenneth Clark. Of Raphael's designs for the Sistine tapestries, Lord Clark remarks in Civilisation,
"The apostles were poor men, their hearers a cross-section of common
humanity. Raphael has made them uniformly handsome and noble
. . . the convention by which the great events in biblical or secular
history could be enacted only by magnificent physical specimens,
handsome and well-groomed, went on for a long time -- till the
middle of the nineteenth century. Only a very few artists -- perhaps
only Rembrandt and Caravaggio in the first rank -- were independent
enough to stand against it." This nobility of Raphael, coupled with
the historical literalism that Vasari first ascribed to Filippo Lippi,
"of making use of carefully studied . . . antiquities," only needed
the development of mass production to produce the popular religious
art that western culture knows today. This was provided at about the
same time -- around 1500 -- by two other giants of the Renaissance,
Albrecht Dürer and Luca della Robbia. Both men contributed to the
technical side of popularizing art, and della Robbia's sugary putti

would provide a pattern for four-and-a-half centuries of saccharine copies.

Yet aesthetic name-calling dodges the problems of popular Christian art, for the popular arts do answer the needs of many devout people, in addition to answering the semi-political requirements of conformity and day-to-day ritual sustenance of the church establishments. The placid and sentimental faces provide for the communicants a feeling of repose, and more important, a hope for eternal repose in the cradle of the church. The faces in the pictures may be as innocuous as the womb, but then, Freud has shown us that the womb is also a popular place. The well-groomed magnificence, the detached superiority to worldly affairs of the images gives every communicant a powerful friend, a spiritual aristocrat to be his lovely barrister in heaven. And the clarity of light, the simplicity of composition shed off theological obscurities like so many scales of dandruff.

Obscurity is an important consideration in popular religious art. The Council of Trent, as we have seen, in 1563 proscribed against anything "disorderly . . . or confusedly arranged." A score of years later, this was spelled out more explicitly by Cardinal Gabriele Paleotti, the Bishop of Bologna. Paleotti's treatment of the question of obscurity in religious art is all worth reading, but this is the nub of it: "One of the main praises that we give to a writer or a practitioner of any liberal art is that he knows how to explain his ideas clearly, and that even if his subject is lofty and difficult, he knows how to make it plain and intelligible to all by his easy discourse. We can state the same of the painters in general, all the more because his works are used mostly as books for the illiterate, to whom we must always speak openly and clearly." As with popular politicians who want to make things "perfectly clear," by obscuring the obscurities, that is to say, by suppressing the ambiguities, so canny religious men have realized that obscurity is an enemy of conformity, and it must be suppressed. This restriction of artistic interpretation was to produce some rather spirited legal hearings for Veronese and El Greco, but the constrictions were hardly necessary for the anonymous producers of popular art, for they have long known that the obscure, the unfamiliar, the indirect, the ambivalent simply do not sell. On the other hand, the sub-conscious and the mythical may sell. In either event, the people's sanction is the final arbiter;

meanings that may seem obscure or deviant to a cultivated person, may strike straight through to the Jungian sub-conscious of the common viewer, and, with the infra-rationality that characterizes mythic understanding, may express ambiguities and obscurities far below the comprehension of the Bishop of Bologna.

This most certainly is the case with the sacred heart chromos. Unbecoming they may be, but their clarity of expression is direct. Passion, pain, sacrifice are the message, and whereas the subtlety of the same message as it is embodied in Michelangelo's Pietá could be blunted to the untutored mind by its elevation and its eloquently quiet psychology, the bleeding, tortured, humiliated, beating flaming cardiac cases obscure nothing of the message. The sacred heart attribute also moves easily from the Virgin Mother to her Son, and often, to prevent any possibility of misinterpretation, the Holy Subject will be depicted as pointing to the heart. In spite of all this obviousness, however, the context within which all these images are found is calm and easy, and the hearts are surrounded by faces that are disconcertingly, sometimes even ludicrously, uninvolved, their expressions ranging from bland, to coy, to vaguely baffled. This particular bloody image is relatively new, of course, but the popular dwelling on blood imagery and implied violence is an older tradition. Gothic crucifixes are often marked by gruesome and terrifying flow of blood from the crown of thorns and from the heavily emphasized stigmata. Iberian and Latin American religious paintings, in particular, increased rather than diminished the torrent. The Iberian bloodiness is a fact, that's clear, but its origins are undoubtedly so complexly mixed out of trickles from the Gothic, and from the Inquisition; from the guilts, fears and passions of Loyola, from Iberias's five centuries of domination by Muslims, and from the remote capillaries of Carthaginian gods and neolithic fertility rituals, that the transfusions into the blood of the saviour are subjects for a volume in itself. From Minoan bull to Papal Bull is a long haul, with much blood spilt along the way. The influences, then, are obscured, but the impact is not, or at any rate it has not been obscured until very recent times, when a contemporary religious painter by the name of Chambers, converted the sacred heart into a demure neon glow, and changed the attitude of the hands of the B.V.M. from unabashed pointing, to a modest covering of the passionate symbol. Indeed, the expression of the hands is closer to Botticelli's

135

Venus than it is to the sacred heart tradition. The Chambers painting reproductions are by far outselling older Catholic popular icons
in the United States, and the reasons for their popularity are mani-
fold. Partly gentility, partly ecumenism, partly embarrassment at
religious fervor, and partly, I think, an uneasiness at displaying the
flagrant minority stigmata in middle class Protestant suburbia are
influences that may all contribute to the suppression of the bloody
icons in the popular minds and homes.

The sacred heart image is one aspect of the popularization of Raphael, although it is not what Vasari admired and Kenneth Clark de-
plored. Their concern was with the pervasiveness of Raphael in the
cultivated tradition, as can be clearly exemplified in a madonna to
be found in the Philbrook Museum of Tulsa, painted by the minor
academician, Felice Schiavoni around 1850. The triangular structure
of Raphael's central groups are there; along with it, the quietly
enraptured face of the madonna, but the infants have become pret-
tied up like foreshadowing of Shirley Temple, and the background has
developed the historical-geographical literalism that has served to
divorce European religious experience from the contemporary scene in
countless palm-strewn, mosque-littered views of the Holy Land ever
since the art academies began to elevate historical painting to the
highest level of culture. In popular chromos and Christmas cards, the
message has shifted from eternal truth to travelogue. It is this literalism that caused Ralph Waldo Emerson, in his Divinity School Address, to castigate theologians for dwelling with a noxious persistence
on the person of Jesus.

Emerson can serve to broaden the scope of my consideration of religious art, for my remarks up to now may suggest that the popularization of religious images through mass production is a Roman Catholic
phenomenon -- and a rather outdated one at that, what with modern
Catholicism revolutionizing the church and its ornaments. Such is
not the case, for regardless of how theologically iconoclastic Prot-
estantism has been and continues to be, even the most fundamentalist
of sects today are paralleled by an ecumenical mass-produced sub-
cultural religion, marked by such things as plastic Jesus-images for
automobile dashboards (the Catholics have the B.V.M. and the officially spurious St. Christopher to guide their cars), and bumper stickers designed by the publishers to the Church of God "for the purpose

of making automobiles as Nahum's Chariots" (at forty dollars per set, as Christian Century reported in deploring tones). In a recent visit to a religious goods store of Protestant orientation, I noted that although Raphael and della Robbia are only sporadically evident, the Renaissance still dominates in the popularized works of Leonardo's Last Supper and Albrecht Dürer's Praying Hands. More ubiquitous, however, is the Pre-Raphaelite William Holman Hunt, whose painting, The Light of the World (1851-1855), is familiar (by association, as we shall see) to every Protestant from his Sunday School books and basements, often becoming the focal point of many iconoclastic homes.

The Light of the World possessed a richness of significance for popular cultural studies from the time of its very inception, for Holman Hunt wrote of that moment: "To paint the picture life size, as I should have desired, would then have forbidden any hope of sale." Religion may be the bread of life to humanity, but for a religious artist, religion is also just plain bread. There is a further irony in Holman Hunt's plaint, for had he eternal copyright on his picture, his royalties must run close to Moses' for writing Exodus. At a deeper level, however, Hunt's designation as an artist as Pre-Raphaelite -- he credits himself with the coining of the term for the whole Brotherhood of Millais, Rossetti, Ford Madox Brown and other peripheral members -- demands some explication. The historical period before Raphael, of course, places one also pre-Reformation, but it is additionally analogous to the primitivistic strivings of the Protestant reformers for regaining the structure and simplicity and evangelism of the primitive church. In extreme forms, as among the American colonial Puritans, the return to fundamentals led to a total purging of icons and symbols from church and home, and that purgation remained effective until the past century, when the popular mass-produced sub-religions developed, probably as outgrowths of illustrated Sunday-school books. Lutherans and Anglicans, however, rarely went to the extremes, and what with Dürer, and later Rembrandt, as practitioners of mass-produced Protestant art, the Christian art tradition is as venerable for Protestants as it is for Catholics.

This religious primitivism, of course, is not the real basis for Pre-Raphaelite art. It grows, rather, from the concerns felt and expressed by many artists and intellectuals in nineteenth-century Europe about the prostitutions that arose out of mass production, industrialization

and popular culture, the concerns exhibiting some of their greatest
manifestations in the Arts and Crafts movement of the Pre-Raphaelites' close associate, William Morris. Once again, though, it is
founded ultimately in the Renaissance. It is not Raphael who is at
fault, for, as Holman Hunt wrote, "There is no need to trace any
failure in Raphael's career; but the prodigality of his productiveness,
and his training of many assistants, compelled him to lay down rules
and manners of work; and his followers, even before they were left
alone, accentuated his poses into postures. They caricatured the
turns of his heads and the lines of his limbs, so that figures were
drawn in patterns. They have twisted companies of men into pyra-
mids, and placed them like pieces on the chess-board of the foreground." These painter-factory travesties we have already seen in
Schiavoni. But the Pre-Raphaelites did not reject all of the Renaissance; rather, they broke the stranglehold by which Italy held High
Art in thrall, just as contemporaneously, Richard Wagner was breaking with Italian opera. The Pre-Raphaelites turned to the Flemish
masters of the Renaissance, and emulated the precisionist delight in
material things of van Eyck, along with the northern artists' welter
of minor-sized symbols, once again parallel to Wagner's tapestries
woven of miniaturized leitmotifs. This kind of symbolic realism is
the intention and it is the fact of Pre-Raphaelite painting, but a
strange transmogrification took place with the mass reproduction of
such works as Light of the World that rendered the Pre-Raphaelite
sunlit glitter as Raphaelite glow. This is because the processes of
offset and chromolithography do the same thing to prints that mono-
type will do: they generalize detail, soften color, and flatten forms,
thereby simplifying masses and etherealizing materialistic reality.
Even the most refined reproductive techniques of today, (with the
probable exception of slide projection) is incapable of communica-
ting the first-hand experience of viewing van Eyck, van der Weyden
or Fouquet. Popular copies of Light of the World, therefore, have
far more similarity to Raphael than to Holman Hunt.

Furthermore, one similarity between early and high Renaissance
painting in both Flanders and Italy contributed to a perennial characteristic of popular religious art, this being the characteristic of
even lighting that illuminates every object in the painting with
nearly equal candlepower, regardless of whether they are in the
foreground or the background. For some reasons, the dramatic

chiaroscuro of Caravaggio, the enshadowed luminosity of Leonardo, and the mystical obscurities of Rembrandt never caught on in popular art. The reasons are not mysterious, however. The least of these is, once more, the manufacturing process that is unfriendly to Leonardo's and Rembrandt's gradual shading. In addition, there is church dogma that opposed the earthy renderings of Biblical subjects by Caravaggio. Allied to this, there are the church proscriptions against obscurity that I have cited before, and, after all, obscure means, covered, in the dark. Finally, the popular audience wants in its religious art just what it wants on its television screen, a picture one can see clearly. Thus, when these considerations are coupled to the limitations of the rotary printing press, the total effect of Light of the World is Raphaelite!

Other changes were wreaked upon Light of the World in popular art. The face of Jesus was extrapolated from Holman Hunt's painting, and combined with popular versions of the German academic painter Heinrich Hofmann, giving Protestants an oval, effeminate, cupids-bow-lipped equivalent to the Catholics' Raphaelite Virgin Mary, not to be altered until recent years when Jesus' hair is mussed into a little-boy manliness, and his bone structure sharpened into a remarkably close likeness of Gregory Peck. -- Jesus Christ, the superstar. And in a version of kitsch, that, like much kitsch art, has a political dimension, Hunt's Jesus is removed from the garden doorway, blown up to a gigantic height and stands on Manhattan Island, to knock, like a sanctified King Kong, on the United Nations Secretariat building.

These last two examples are not mere curiosities. They are the works of the most recent of a triumvirate of America's most famous artists, none of whom has his name in any standard art directory, encyclopedia or Who's Who. Their fame is not only a matter of sales figures, it is a matter of their names having a currency in America that quite possibly touches more people than do the names of Rembrandt, Picasso or even Andrew Wyeth. The outlaw triumvirate of American religious art is Sallman, Anderson and Hook. It is Sallman who painted the 1940 updating of Light of the World, as well as the standard face of Jesus for the mid-twentieth century. It is Anderson who painted the Prince of Peace U. N. version of Light of the World, and it is Hook who is coming up fast on the inside with the Gregory Peck hip Jesus portraits. This is all outlaw art, having neither the

approval of the art establishment, nor the attention of critics, nor even the realization of its existence by the cultivated audience. Yet, from border to border in America, there are thousands of people who walk into art stores to buy "a Sallman," or "Hook's Jesus." Thus, in the visual arts, it may be paradoxically true that the majority of patrons of the arts are an outcast "minority." The historical development of this "minority's" image of the Christ is not haphazard, however, because from the time that Sallman removed Hunt's crown from Jesus, there has been a continuous democratization and masculinization of the icon, which may indicate a reduction of divinity in Jesus, or it may indicate a popular version of the elevation of every man to divine dignity, as Michelangelo had elevated man to godlike status on the Sistine ceiling four centuries earlier. Which brings us back to the Renaissance.

Similar adjustments have been made in Leonardo da Vinci's Last Supper, a painting whose ecumenism transcends all denominational lines. In my visit to the religious artifact retail store, I was puzzled to notice something in a large litho of The Last Supper that had previously eluded me. This was an oriental rug on the floor in front of the trestle table. It appeared to me to be an anachronism, but given the fact of fifteenth-century Venetian trade with the Byzantine empire, it seemed possible, if not plausible. Even so, it seemed an intrusion in a High Renaissance fresco, so I hastened to a library to resolve my doubts. The rug, I found, was placed on the floor to cover the hole in the fresco made when a door was cut through the wall below it in the Convent of Santa Maria delle Grazie in Milan. There are worlds of meaning in this oriental rug, for it, more than any other symbol, ties popular mass-produced religious art to the popular folk tradition. Unlike the self-conscious, political manipulation of Holman Hunt's Jesus into Manhattan, and unlike the Madison Avenue manipulation of Jesus' face into that of a superstar, this placing of the rug is a common-sense understandable solution to the problem of what to do with an embarrassing flaw in the floor: cover it with a scatter rug. Earlier, I stated that the variations in folk art are more often the results of the slip of the brush, a short-circuit in the memory, a narrowness of experience, than they are the results of spiritual upheaval of willful self-expression. Such is the case in this manufactured Last Supper, and it gives some of the innocent genuineness that an earthy colonial painter of the Post-Inca Cuzco school gave to a

Holy Family where Joseph busies himself with his carpentry, while
the Mother of God wipes the Christ-child's bare bottom. The latter
example offends, if what we expect is Raphael's other-worldly bam-
bino; while the Last Supper rug offends, if what we expect is a
humanist's scholarly veneration of an art masterpiece. Yet either
of these expectations ignores the real function of religious art, to
be a window to higher realities. Of which, more later.

Returning to the religious art list of All-Time-Greats in the popular
tradition, all that is needed to complete the list is Albrecht Dürer's
Praying Hands. Subtle and less "divine" than the popular works of
Raphael, Hunt and Leonardo, Dürer's drawing has undoubtedly ap-
pealed because of its lack of divinity. They are hands that do not
go beyond human experience. The other popular works may be
realistic, but the Praying Hands is naturalistic. They are not youthful hands and so they probably summon up sentimental associations
of devout parents and grandparents. Moreover, they can satisfy the
deeply-rooted need for an icon even among the most iconoclastic
evangelical of sects, for they represent worship rather than that which
is worshiped. Similar to Praying Hands is Grace, commonly presumed
to be a painting, but in reality a copyrighted posed photograph,
extremely close to the English photographer Henry Peach Robinson's
Day's Work Done (1877) with the common elements of devout old age,
peasant repast and non-liturgical content. Grace is a particularly
good case in point for popular cultural studies, for it is surrounded by
incorrigible misconceptions -- I have had a dealer in religious art
gently but emphatically "correct" my statement that Grace was
originally a black-and-white photograph -- this despite the fact
that the publisher, Augsburg Press of Minneapolis, distributes broadcast a brochure describing the history of Eric Enstrom's photograph.
Like so many phenomena of popular culture, though, the goats-nest
of inter-influences among audience, artist and manufacturers is further disordered by Augsburg's practice of printing Grace on "brush
stroke canvas" paper, presumably because the popular audience may
not ascribe the honorific art to a photograph.

Day's Work Done, Grace and Praying Hands have the advantage of
Protestant non-liturgical appeal. It has been suggested to me by a
publisher of Protestant religious artifacts that Protestant art started
with Gustave Doré, whose Bible Gallery, Divine Comedy and

Paradise Lost were the first real picture books to find their ways
into nineteenth-century homes, doubly bastioned by being Christian
and Cultured, at the same time that the romantic dramatic style of
which Doré was the master among engravers, could excite and titil-
late the most dour of puritans. This suggestion seems valid, for it
provides the medium link that must exist before a Protestant restores
icons to his home's walls; that is, the leap from the Bible as sole
source of religious inspiration to the domestic wall shrine, could not
be possible without the media of the illustrated Bible, the illustrated
religious poem, and, eventually, the secular genre photograph.
Enstrom's Grace, therefore, like the various renditions of Praying
Hands, is a touching, low-keyed and oblique picture that allows the
communicant to relate his act of worship to an icon, and thereby, to
a larger religious community, but without any hint of idol-worship,
the bane of all Protestants. In short, as with all popular religious
icons, Praying Hands and its analogs are capable of maintaining the
sabbath ritual and community in the seclusion of the home. In spite
of these virtues, however, mass production and mass distribution result in the same kind of reduced sharpness and reinterpretation that
make Hunt's Pre-Raphaelite detail into Post-Raphaelite diffusion.
Thus, the veins, the wrinkles, the underlying bone structure that
render Dürer's hands into an abstract investigation into texture and
mass, are lost in the simple anecdotal message implied by the apoc-
ryphal title of the drawing.

Human hands are eloquent. Their eloquence knows no cultural restriction, and even the least demonstrative of cultures cannot escape
the tenderness of a mother's hand, nor can it avoid the communion
of handclasps of lovers, of friends, of parties to a contract, nor of
the records of years and of labors imprinted upon the hands of the
aged. Hands, consequently, provide us with a useful focus for dis-
tinguishing among the various aesthetics, folk, cultivated and popular. This is particularly true in the case of religious arts, for religions abound in hand imagery; the laying on of hands, the benedic-
tion, the stigmata, and so on. In folk culture, the hands are used
unconsciously, while in popular visual arts, hands take on character
primarily from the abortive attempts at depicting a very difficult
subject. Faulty bone articulation, over-simplified wrinkles and
fingernails, and noticeably crowded fingers make folk art. A nineteenth-century Mexican retablo depicting the bleeding hand of

Christ illustrates all of these characteristics. The fingers are reduced
to smooth tubes, devoid of knuckles. The little finger is an extension
of flesh without skeletal support, the thumbnail is marked only by an
outline, and the palm is inadequate in size for the fingers. By contrast, Raphael's Madonna of the Goldfinch (1506) is as much a cele-
bration of the human hand as is Dürer's study. The Virgin's right
hand, gently placed in maternal encouragement on the shoulder of St.
John is a psychological study in itself. Her other hand, holding,
somewhat anachronistically, a book, bespeaks interrupted contemplation more than a dozen pointing fingers could hope to do. The
hands of the two children are the dramatic focus of the painting. The
hand of infant Jesus is timid, but not coy, the hand of John, holding
the bird, no bloodless icon, but bone and muscle in a medium of
gravity and air.

In popular religious artifacts, however, the images of hands are washed
of individuality, both in texture and gesture, and, while remaining
anatomically correct, they become stylized semaphores and cease to
operate as psychological art. Before we condemn them as being signal of Bad Art, though, let us bear in mind that in religious use, it
is not their purpose to represent or to evoke individual acts and responses, but rather their purpose is to produce congruent, predictable
responses.

The study of hands also provides an opportunity to extend this es-
say beyond Christian religious art, for mass production of religious
icons is not only a phenomenon of the western tradition. In Hindu
religious art there are chromos much like those of the Sacred Heart
and the Prince of Peace, with the same garish coloring, the same
heavily emphasized symbols, the same cupid's-bow effeminacy, and
the same reduction of hands to expressionless generalities. And this
is within a cultivated tradition of religious art that has for a millen-
ium and more carried the artistic capabilities of the human hand to
a degree of subtlety only approached by Indonesian and Polynesian
dance, and reaching far, far beyond any western expression. Hindu
religious art is in large part born of dance, and thus, its multiplicity
of images is partly explained by the inability of plastic art to capture
more than one moment of motion. Furthermore, just as twentieth-
century European artists in their efforts to compensate for this static
restriction, have, in painting, produced multiple exposures as in

Duchamp's Nude Descending A Staircase, and in sculpture, the mobile, so in Hindu art, the stopped motion of dance has been represented by surplus arms. In the Siva Nataraja -- the Dancing Shiva -- therefore, it is possible to express the terrible complexity of God, Man and eternity by using four mudras (hands) and hastas (hands and arms) at once. So, there is one right hand bearing the drum upon which is beaten the primordial note of creation; another right hand held palm forward in the pose of Abhaya Hasta, the gesture of protection; one left hand bearing Agni, the sacred fireball of sacrifice; the other left hand in the pose of Danda Hasta, the easy, abandoned, yet powerful grace of the lolling trunk of the elephant -- the associations with Ganesha, the beloved elephant-headed benign god, being implied with a human grace. The significance of the pose does not end here, for Shiva's right foot tramples the evil dwarf Muyalagam, while his left foot is raised in perfect balance, showering grace by negation, as it does not choose to trample anything but evil. This, then, is Shiva, in this gift-giving aspect, yet Shiva is the Destroyer aspect of the tripartite godhead. The icon, therefore, is complex beyond reason, and yet it represents no more than one-ninth of the entirety of God. Surely this is too obscure for the Bishop of Bologna and his illiterate parishioners. Indeed, it appears that it is also too obscure, complex and ambivalent for the average Hindu.

The popular aspects of god that appeal to the Hindus are not those of Shiva Nataraja, but the far more benign, generous and humane aspects of Ganesha, who presides with the combined girth and jollity of Dumbo and Santa Claus; of the Lord Krishna, who is reborn in annual ritual as a Christ-like baby, with the continuous promise of his tenth metamorphosis (Krishna being the human avator of Vishnu) as Kalki, or Vishnu of the White Horse and deliverance; and of Shiva in his two-armed, contemplative, yogic aspect. It is this last that particularly speaks of the universality of popular mass-produced religious art, because the face of Shiva, like the face of Jesus, is made to surrender both its majesty and its flesh-and-blood humanity, to become an expression of simpering, indulgent maternalism. Likewise, Krishna, as with the baby Jesus, is converted to a pretty, harmless, walking doll.

But once again, my modifiers are unjust, and I am guilty of criticizing "good religion" as "bad art." It must never be forgotten that the

144

popular icon is not an egotistic window on humanity, but an anonymous window on the hope of salvation. Shiva and Krishna for devout
Hindus, like Madonna and Child for devout Christians, are representative friendly barristers in Heaven, not one-of-kind museum-pieces.

The art of India is useful to popular culture studies for another reason,
because it casts more light on the tradition of mass production; or
rather, it casts more shadows. India has had a long tradition of
standardized religious art, second only to the art of ancient Egypt in
longevity, and a veritable granddaddy to dogmatic Christian traditions. Indeed, the artists of Indian religious expression are lost in
antiquity. The traditions and techniques that they developed in dance
and in ragas and in sculpture have long since been codified. Thus,
in the fifty-seventh chapter of the Brhatsamhita, we find such dicta
as: "The goccha [dimple in the center of the upper lip] is one-half
angula [a unit of measurement] in length, the mouth being four angulas in length. When the latter is closed, it is one-and-a-half angulas in width, it being three angulas wide, when open. . . . The
feet are twelve angulas in length and six in breadth; the second toe
is three angulas long. . . . The rest of the toes should be made less
by one-eighth, in succession. . . ." In a similar ancient book, the
Pratimamana-laksanam, the feet of female goddesses are patterned
thus: "The toes are said to be like a green mango in appearance, the
top of the feet should be made like the back of a tortoise; the toes are
said to be similar to the feet of a swan. The feet should be made flat
and level and the nails, of the form of oyster shells." Add to this the
fact that, as S. K. Ray explains in The Folk-Art of India, metal-
workers are of the lowest castes, i.e., outcastes; there is no amateur,
independent, or progressive art tradition in India. That is, unlike
Japan, where amateur art has long been the dignified pastime of the
highly educated, and unlike post-medieval Europe, where artists have
been given wide latitude in self-expression, along with tickets for
admission to the highest levels of society, in India, the production
of art works has been relegated to a caste having no prerogatives for
self-expression and few opportunities for contact with a changing
society and a changing ethos. Consequently, the methods of western
industrialization, when they were applied to the mass production of
religious icons, could only convert firmly entrenched styles into
depersonalized assembly-line products.

Still, along side of assembly-line products, the over-populated eastern nations have retained hereditary and traditional skills of individual craftsmanship, and thus, bronzes, paintings, ivory and woodcarvings done by the oriental equivalents of European master-guilds continue; but surely mass production will proceed inexorably to destroy these time-consuming, low-output craftsmen, as it has done throughout the western world, but this destruction may take place without the influence of William Morris, Elbert Hubbard and Walter Gropius to give high-caste redirection to the course of industrialized craftsmanship. The brahmins must get their hands dirty, or cultivated art in India may die.

But this melancholy prophecy is not to the point. The point is that it is entirely possible for cultivated art to exist without progressive change. It is the western way to define cultivated art as a dialectic, that is, to find quality and cultivation in the combat zone between stasis and progress, between academy and rebel. It is further the western way to define cultivated art in individualistic expression rather than in the products of copy cats. These are the attitudes that make mass-produced traditional arts repellent, by definition, to the cultivated consumer. Yet, if we examine the arts of India, Yucatan, China, Egypt and the European Middle Ages, we find that great art is often popular art, that it is produced by artisans, not Artists, and that it is designed to correspond to formulas and prototypes. It changes, slowly, of course, and probably not in the office of progressive leader for the culture, but as follower of the changing ethos. But in these exotic cultures, individual craftsmanship permits delicacy and intricacy, and shapes and lines that derive from the artisan's hand. It is that individual touch of the hand that makes much of this popular art attractive to us: the curve in slip clay that tells us a woman's thumb has been there; the easy heft of a wooden image that makes our hands to feel the grasp of other hands across the ages; the accidental air pocket in a casting that brings us one to one in the brotherhood of fallibility: these are the intrinsic humanistic contents of popular handcrafted arts that are shared with folk art, and with careful self-consciousness, with cultivated art.

But industrial mass production does something different when it presses the popular arts into its rotaries. The touch is gone, and this disturbs the cultivated consumer. Unless he is an unmitigated snob, though,

146

he is not opposed to mass production. This, thanks to the high aesthetics of Baskerville at his type-font, William Morris at his looms, Toulouse-Lautrec at his lithographic stones, Aalto at his plywood factories, does not spell the end of cultivated art. Nonetheless, the cultivated patron of mass-produced art is not really a consumer of mass art, because he demands limited editions, and is disturbed by popularity. (We will hear more of limited edition mass-produced art in the next chapter). The popular consumer, however, is not disturbed by massed editions, nor does he seem to be disturbed by the lack of the human touch. That is, he is innocent of the techniques of the human hand. In spite of this, it is my contention that the popular arts do have a human touch. The human touch that the popular consumer discerns is not technical, though, but mythic, ideological, and psychological. Popular religious artifacts, consequently, communicate by satisfaction alone, not by understanding or analysis. The popular consumer says yes or he says no. He does not say why? Nor does he say whence? The popular consumer's affirmative response implies that there is something in this totality to satisfy some needs for which he has no words beyond yes, I like it, I will take it.

It is at this point that Levi-Strauss' analogy of music and myth as forms of universal expression and communication is helpful. They are equally inarticulated, though both speak to humanity. Further, it is at this point that my earlier political analogy can be helpful, for politicians and mass-artists tell their audiences, I will make myself into what you need. They do not say, take me as I am, for that would be the way of the artist-hero. And there is another similarity between politics and popular religious art to be considered, this being the absence of aesthetic standards in the cultivated tradition of the arts. There are degrees of comprehension and sophistication in popular culture, and popular culture will sometimes produce poetry from politics, and art from icons, as we can see in Lincoln's Second Inaugural Address and della Robbia's plaster putti. Nevertheless, the degrees of comprehension in religion do not require aesthetic judgments. As a particularly lucid exposition of these degrees, Benjamin Walker's description in The Hindu World is applicable to all religions and, by extension, to political ideologies. He says, "The highest form of devotion is the worship of Brāmā in his purest form, Brahma without attributes based on realization of the identity of self with

147

Brahma. The second is the worship of Brahma with attributes. . . as creator, ruler, provider, Lord of Life and Death. The third and most popular form is the worship of a prafīka or symbol of the diety. This form is for those who are incapable of higher meditative worship. The symbol may be a picture, an idol, or the sun or any natural phenomenon, and all Hindus, even those who perform the higher forms, worship God in the prafīka form as well."

Not a word about aesthetic beauty. Indeed, since the ultimate devotion is formless, how can it be art? Yet, the ultimate religious experience is similar to what Bernard Berenson calls "the aesthetic moment." In Aesthetics and History, Berenson says,". . . the aesthetic moment is that flitting instant, so brief as to be almost time-less, when the spectator is at one with the work of art. . . . He ceases to be his ordinary self, and the . . . actuality is no longer outside himself. The two become one entity. . . . It is as if he had been initiated into illuminating, exalting, formative mysteries. In short, the aesthetic moment is a moment of mystic vision."

In mystical experience, therefore, (though not in mystical meaning) art and religion are one. And the two are related in that art is often an expression of religion, and in that religion often uses art as a vehicle for devotion. Furthermore, at times the aesthetic moment and the religious experience may occur simultaneously within an indi-vidual psyche, but, since both experiences transcend the individual's existence, how are we ever to know what is divine and what is aes-thetic?

With that question mark the similarity ends. For this investigation into popular religious arts has brought me to two unexpected conclu-sions. First, there are no tools to be acquired through the study of the cultivated arts that really prepare one to criticize justly popular religious art; it is nearly all "bad art." But this is the merest gallery criticism, shallow and irrelevant, and evading the function of popu-lar religious art. The converse situation, surprisingly, is not a mirror image, however, for the true religious communicant may be well equipped to pierce through all the superficialities of a Great Art Work to perceive its spiritual essence, and to judge it either a true icon or false; yet, on the other hand, his experience with popu-lar religious art will not prepare him for any formal judgments about

148

art as art, and it may not ready him at all for the "aesthetic moment."

The second unexpected conclusion, is that popular religious art, cheap and transient, is throw-away art because it is so profound: the physical object was never the object of worship. The physical object is only the icon, the window, the prafīka, the medium between the human being and higher meanings. Aesthetic art, on the other hand, is not disposable, because the object is the deity. The lost plays of Euripides, the lost temple of Solomon, the lost chord of Sullivan are lost, all, lost, and can be productive of no aesthetic experiences. But cast-off pratīka are no loss to the seeker after religious generation and regeneration, for he desires to lose his identity in God, not in a work of art. The true communicant does not need Raphael or Robert Shaw; Sallman and Dale Evans will do quite as well, and in a pinch he can nail two sticks into a cross and hum Rock of Ages for himself. The desert winds have blown away a thousand sand-paintings, but the profound ambiguities of Navajo religion go on in new sand-paintings. In traditional Africa, carved images of generations and of weeks past are cast aside when their meanings are gone, for no deity resides in the wood; it is only in Nommo, the naming of the piece of wood, and in Kuntu, the giving it a form generally appropriate to its name, that the wood becomes worthy. And when the particular Nommo is no longer needed, the wood is just wood, Kintu, a mere thing.

Kuntu, sand-painting, pratīka, chromo, plastic Jesus: all are things only, whose beauty is but an accident of the clock's moment; but they are things whose function derives from meanings named into them by humanity. Icons may be good, but they are temporal, and can be cast off by religious man, if they get in the way of his striving for immortality and the continuance of his race. Thus, Leonardo da Vinci wrote: "And you, O Man, who will discern in this work of mine the wonderful works of Nature, if you think it would be a criminal thing to destroy it, reflect how much more criminal it is to take the life of a man; and if this, his external form appears to thee marvelously constructed, remember that it is nothing as compared with the soul that dwells in the structure; for that, indeed, be it what it may, is a thing divine."

God may indeed love man's artifacts, not because there are so many

149

of them, but because so many men have discovered the eternal within the works of man.

Middlebrow Arts and
Souvenir   Aesthetics

In modern times, since the Renaissance, the separation of the cultivated arts and artists from the popular arts, from the popular artisans,
and from the popular audience has been the rule, despite the several
attempts at rapprochement that provide some of the more stimulating
spots in the history of arts in society. The predominant trend of
separation started in the early sixteenth century, with the development of artists' academies. Originally, the academies were designed
to circumvent the medieval guild system, where artists continued to be
equated with artisans, and where young artists were limited to mechanical apprenticeship, typically doing only manual work, rough sculpture and the like. Academies, or "the academy," therefore, started
in answer to the artists' needs for more freedom, for more elevated
artistic goals, and for a more rational approach to art education.

This original purpose is considerably different from the usual "myth
of the academy," where the academicians are viewed as the stulti-
fying "Bad Guys" of art history who opposed all that was progressive
and creative. These mythic Bad Guys were the anti-Impressionists,
the anti-Post-Impressionists, the anti-Expressionists, the anti-any-
thing avantgarde. Yet regardless of the general validity of the myth

during the past hundred years, it remains true that no reaction against the academies appeared among artists until the dawn of the nineteenth century. Therefore, it would appear that the academies served their original purpose of freeing and dignifying both art and artists for at least two hundred years.

The Renaissance artists and their heirs wanted and needed separation from popular craft guilds to secure greater liberty for themselves. Nonetheless, their liberty was guaranteed only by insisting upon an elite separation from the popular majority. By the eighteenth century, a normal academy structure had developed that underscores this separation. At the top of the academy was a royal or aristocratic protector, and group of honorary members -- connoisseurs and dilettantes of noble class --, below that a teaching staff and artist members -- Academicians --, and finally, at the bottom, students. Later developments in the history of academies in art might be interesting to pursue here, but I wish mainly to emphasize that they have been a major force in enforcing the separation of the artist from the popular culture of his day. Academies still exist, but the institutional academies have been largely replaced in America by what might be characterized more loosely as "the establishment," a complicated but secure coterie of New York galleries, major museums, wealthy patrons and select publications and critics. My use of the terms "academy" and "establishment" includes all these ideas of sanctioned elitism.

From time to time throughout modern history, artists have courted the popular crafts and artisans in attempts to restore the artist to his pre-academy medieval position as one who incorporated beauty into everyday craftsmanship, rather than as one who produced certified beauty to embellish the residences of the elite. Among the "guild movements" that attempted to restore the connection between art and daily life are those of William Morris, in the 1860's, and of the ensuing English Arts and Crafts movement that carried on into this century with such American artistic do-it-yourselfers as Elbert Hubbard, whose Roycroft colony in East Aurora, New York produced handcrafted books and furnishings. Today, we look back at those attempts to incorporate the artist into society as romantically impractical, however interesting they may seem to intellectuals. Such "guild movements" are in that respect very much in the mode of

Whitman's poetry for the common man, but in this case, the overall
influence of this sort of union of craftsman and artist is not so remote
as some might think, for our whole "modern" life-style is no more
than an undiminished reverberation from the more recent attempt at
the same thing at Walter Gropius' Bauhaus, well over half-a-century
ago. Gropius, in 1965, stated the essence of his lifetime mission of
bringing arts and people together: "There is a widespread heresy
that art is just a useless luxury," he wrote. "This is one of our fatal
legacies from a generation which arbitrarily elevated some of its
branches above the rest as the 'Fine Arts,' and in so doing robbed
all of their basic identity and common life. The typical embodiment
of the l'art pour l'art mentality, and its chosen instrument, was 'the
Academy.' By depriving handicrafts and industry of the informing
services of the artists the academies drained them of their vitality,
and brought about the artist's complete isolation from the community
. . . . What we [at the Bauhaus] preached in practice was the common citizenship of all forms of creative work and their logical inter-
dependence on one another in the modern world."

These are criticisms and missions with which we must all agree, and
yet, ironically, what the Bauhaus inadvertantly produced was a
dominant academy of the century that turned out modishly barren
products for wealthy patrons and image-conscious industry. Business
corporations in particular seem always to apply Bauhaus to the front
office rather than to their products, thereby missing the point that
Gropius really intended: functionalism is not rationale for standardized formal design, rather, it is a means toward "the aesthetic satisfaction of the human soul" through "the common citizenship of all
form of creative work." The common citizenship of Gropius' intent,
though, became an uncommon elite in practice.

Something is awry here, just as something was awry with craft movements of William Morris and Elbert Hubbard. All these men, like
Karl Marx, recognized that in some way machinery and industrialism
had alienated the worker from his product, but unlike Marx, who
reasoned from the alienation along economic and political lines,
these men reasoned along lines of design. In the case of Gropius,
good design was to develop in alliance with mass production, while
in the case of the Arts and Crafts leaders, the design was to develop
in opposition to mass production. Yet, in both cases, the results

were only some more "-isms" in the history of the Fine Arts, rather
than effective revolutions in worker-aesthetics. The worker in the
Ford plant may turn out parts for a sleekly designed functionmobile,
but the automotive designer of that Ford is a graduate of M. I. T.
The worker's art and poetry is found on greeting cards and church
programs, the designer's in the Whitman and Gropius he studied at
M. I. T.

The artist who sets out to create art of the people invariably creates
art for the people, and quite clearly, the people don't want art that
is created for them in particular; they want art that is real, certified
art. Greeting card verse is not only a "useless luxury," but it is
elevated and idealistic, as "Fine Arts" should be, full of abstract
thought and lofty sentiments. The popular art patron, in short, has
become the greatest supporter of the elevated goals of the old academies of arts! How did we come to this state of affairs?

Mainly, what has gone awry in the theories that seek to end the alienation of product and people, is that they neglect the fact that the
popular audience are consumers of arts, not producers. The consumer
of arts is part of the mass patronage of the arts. The same industry
that alienated "mass-man" from creative involvement in the output
of his assembly line also made available to him the arts of the world.
The popular mind, therefore, is not as intellectuals have thought, a
shadow of the medieval guild craftsman; the popular mind is a cinemascope projection of the Medici and the Popes of Rome, whose
relation to art was not creation, but patronage and selection.

The so-called "alienation" of artisan and product, therefore, developed at the same time that industry was producing a mass of consumers.
These consumers, who were formerly peasants, serfs, chattels, ten-
ants, wage-slaves, conscripts, dependents and debtors, did not join
the middle-class to achieve more and better folk-culture, but to win
for themselves a piece of the upper-class action. Their desire to
partake of the elite arts is a major reason for the development of
middlebrow arts in opposition to the attempts to exalt guilds and folk
arts. But this brings my argument to another sort of attempt at rapprochement between artist and popular audience, this time not like
the Bauhaus' courting of guild-skills, but rather the courting of artists by the nouveau-riche consumer. This middle-class consumer (or

patron) has the desires of the old upper-class patron, and subscribes
to the exclusive definitions that the academy provides so eagerly.
Still, this consumer (or patron) also retains the aesthetics of his
folk-popular background. For him art should demonstrate clearly
that it is different from the humdrum of everyday, and for him, art
should state simply whatever its message may be.

But here I must pause to serve notice that the illustrations of middle-
class popular arts will not have the earthy democracy of serial television, professional wrestling, Sears Roebuck catalogs, first-grade
readers, or truck-tire fences. The aspect of the popular mind of
which I am speaking now is more readily perceived at the upper-
income portions of the social-economic-educational scale. This aspect of the popular mind is that which Russell Lynes named the "upper-
middlebrow." It is marked by a striving for exclusiveness and sophistication that is handicapped by the lack of a substantial background,
training and life-style in conscious art patronage. It is expressed in
material goods, trappings, holdings and collections. This upper-
middlebrow syndrome became a subject of popular concern in the
1950's -- a decade that seems now to be accused of possessing an
oafish naiveté concerning its materialism -- but a decade, nonetheless, that was in reality deeply disturbed about its prosperity. The
Fifties demonstrated their uneasiness by the immense popularity of
such works of the decade as David Riesman's The Lonely Crowd, William Whyte's The Organization Man, Vance Packard's The Status
Seekers, Russell Lynes' The Tastemakers and C. Wright Mills' White
Collar: The American Middle Classes. Mills' book described the
"status panic" among white-collar workers, those people whose prestige had been reduced by a number of factors, including such things
as the raising of wage-worker incomes, the increasing number of
high-school graduates, the decline of a population of immigrant
origin, and so on. "All these tendencies for white-collar occupations to sink in prestige," Mills concluded, "rest upon the numerical
enlargement of the white-collar strata and the increase in prestige
which the wage-workers have enjoyed. If everybody belongs to the
fraternity, nobody gets any prestige from belonging."

Which brings together two evolutionary strains that constitute the
class of new art patrons. The one evolutionary strain is that of the
formerly disenfranchised persons who are struggling upward; the other

is that of the formerly secure middle-class persons whose prestige is under attack from below. Together, these persons need to possess indicators of their arrival and of their welcome into elevated classes. To put all of this into a simple category, it is the phenomenon of the nouveau-riche and their conspicuous consumption.

Or of bourgeois gentilhomme. Either term indicates that this is neither a recent nor a local phenomenon. From Aristophanes to Petronius, from Molière to Dickens, from Howells to Veblen, from Sinclair Lewis to Jiggs and Maggie, from Riesman to The Beverly Hillbillies, the man-on-the-make for membership in cultivated society has been an object of attention, occasionally of sympathetic study, but most often, of ridicule and disparagement. At best he is a feist masquerading as a thoroughbred; at worst, he believes his own masquerade. The saddest note, however, is the too-frequent denial of beginnings, the turning of the back upon the traditional or popular culture from which the new patron came. This produces the kind of tension that is best exemplified in Jiggs and Maggie. Most often, though, Jiggs' longing for the peasant joys at Dinty Moore's are suppressed, and Maggie's insistence on attending the opera is the salient feature of this nouveau audience.

Because for this audience, art must be exclusive, but lawful. It must also be conspicuously expensive, yet within one's means. At a folk-popular level, this sort of exclusive ostentation is satisfied by souvenir bumper stickers: "We've Been to Disney World." For the upper-middlebrow bumper stickers will not do, but commercial institutions are nevertheless ready to package for this audience conspicuously expensive exclusive lawful art works. They have been at it for a long time, but as a mass phenomenon, it doubtless dates back only to the late nineteenth-century, when numerous economic, technological and social developments made possible a large audience for elite culture. An especially exemplary sampling can be made from the art books that were souvenir outgrowths of the World's Columbian Exposition in Chicago in 1893. For exclusive ostentation, they qualify from their brontosaurian size: one, The Book of the Fair, by Hubert Howe Bancroft (who has been called a "history-factory" rather than a historian) is composed of ten volumes, with a total of one thousand glossy pages, each page 17 by 22 inches, with a surface area of 2.6 square feet apiece -- which comes to about one-sixth

acre of unwieldy culture. These unreadable books are exemplary not only because of their ostentation, but because of their lawfulness as well. The art of the Chicago World's Fair was one of the last great crestings of official academic art. A World's Fair is a best-foot-forward occasion and those who looked at the art at the Fair could rest assured that it was the very best of the very finest arts of all nations.

Another art book that was an outgrowth of the Chicago World's Fair and which was somewhat better sized for the parlor table is Art and Artists of All Nations. Here a tooled leather binding encloses four hundred glossy pages of photographic reproductions of academic art from all European countries and from the United States. A quick glance at the pages of Art and Artists of All Nations shows an apparent rubbish heap of sentimental genre paintings and monumental historical scenes, but more sympathetic study suggests that although one's first impression is eminently correct, there is a considerable range of quality. No pictures show utter absence of technical facility; and although some paintings in Art and Artists of All Nations are rather poor, they were not accepted by the Columbian Exposition. A. Lins' A Song Without Words is probably the worst of the lot, with grotesque china-doll children racing toward the viewer. Were the children cut out completely, a fairly competent street scene with grander divisions of space would result, but of course, it would lose its sentimental appeal. However, A Song Without Words provides a fine whipping-boy, since it is guilty of virtually all the faults of turn of the century academic art, faults that might be summarized as over-explicitness. The painting has too much, too clearly explained; it is words without song.

Another German picture, similar in subject, which was exhibited at the Fair is Once Upon A Time, by Herman Kaulbach. It is vastly superior to Lins' painting in technique, yet it exhibits the same fault in clearer language. Academic art schools had always strived for ideal human features, but even so, Kaulbach's children, unlike Lins', possess individuality. The artist does not dodge the problems of complex grouping, and the background does not immediately obtrude upon the center of interest. Nonetheless it is visually over-explicit. The door handle, the crossbow and the little girl's keys are detailed to the point of fracturing the composition into three

157

irrelevant pockets of interest. And the storyteller, perched precar-
iously on a chest which apparently dissolves into the door, has put
on his story-telling clothes to have his picture painted. Historical
authenticity was another of the primary goals of academic art, and
so it is not surprising that the man's costume is the visual subject of
the work, but its detail cancels out the eminently successful genre
situation which the facial expression evoke. This painting is probably a good qualitative mean for the other works in this middle-brow
art book, although its sentimental subject matter is representative of
maybe only a quarter of the works included. Languid ladies in Whist-
ler costumes account for another large segment, as do harem scenes,
cavalry charges, bucolic scenes, marine studies, and interior genre
paintings. In purpose, these paintings, like later popular movies and
television, are intended variously to produce humor, tenderness,
occasionally titillation by means of dishabille and bronze brassieres,
and rarely, melancholy; or to inform the viewer about costume, cus-
toms or historical events; or to evoke some genteel social protest.
Many are very fine paintings; several have been resurrected in recent
years along with the renewed sympathy with nineteenth-century art.
Even so, Art for Art's sake is not here, at least as we understand art
as an expressionist or intellectual abstraction, but there is something
here far more in keeping with the taste of the popular mind. This is
technique for technique's sake.

Techniques of verisimilitude have been admired by the middle-class
popular audience from the birth of both the middle class and scientific
perspective. I would hesitate to suggest a causal relationship between
Renaissance audience tastes and Renaissance painter's techniques,
simply because the technical advances of fifteenth-century painting
are so obviously related to a stimulating climate of inquiry, exploration and exploitation of human potential. The technical developments in Renaissance painting are hardly the same thing as pandering
to the realistic minds of the middle-class. There was, however, a
happy relationship between artist and patron-consumer, for both were
pleased at the "photographic" renderings of details and scientifically
derived illusions of space and color. Dutch florals, local landscapes,
and recognizable interior anecdotes provide one perfect instance of
the tastes of a wealthy, but broadly based middle-class patronage.
The popular bulk of Dutch painting is what I am referring to here;
Vermeer's stunning probings into pure light and air are exceptional;

158

Rembrandt's deep studies of the human spirit, exceptions.

The aesthetic of the middle-brow patron that is voiced is "I know what I like," but the oft-stated rejoinder of critics, "You like what you know," in no way reverses the validity of the stated popular aesthetic, or of the popular patronage. The middlebrow popular patron does know what he likes. He wants things that will announce his cultivation; he likes things that are real, unambiguous, clear and simple. Wants and likes are intertwined in the desire for things of monetary value, art as investment. The primary subject here is the visual arts, but it may help to illustrate the likes and wants of this patron with examples from the audio arts. The vast technology and industry of aural verisimilitude which we call "high fidelity" developed from the desire of patrons of concert music for accurate reproduction that would not distort the aesthetic experience. The popular patron was drawn quickly toward the hi-fi equipment, which promised verisimilitude, was undeniably cultivated, showed cost and quality in woofer size and in the variety of dials, and was probably a good investment, at least in trade-in value. But what has happened aesthetically as a result of hi-fi advances? First, the concert music patrons who started it all still will buy a Fürtwängler, a Gigli, a Bix, a Caruso in preference to certain hi-fi recordings because they can distinguish between fidelity and truth. Second, the recording industry provided art-works that would utilize the high fidelity machines with clear and simple beauty: not only in stereo recordings of planes, trains and racing cars, not only in cascading violins of Montavani and Melochrino playing "the themes" from La Boheme and Taras Bulba, but most significantly, in new art forms that span the scale of tastes from the most stereotyped mass pop music for teen-agers to the most avant-garde of concert aesthetes. These include such things as the floor-shaking enhanced basses in country-western music, composite pop performances from sixteen-track recorders, rediscovered and revitalized hi-fi symphonists like Mahler and Berlioz, and experimental electronic "serious" music. The middle-man is still in the middle, however, with tastes ranging from enhanced Montavani "Hits of the Fifties" to the 1812 Overture with real guns, real church-bells, real Russian choirs. Technical quality is good in all of this, and just as the Hollywood filmmaking technical quality continues to put many "art-films" to shame, real hi-fi can make an actual live performance of music seem not quite quadrasonic. Which it isn't.

In respect to technical quality, therefore, there has been a continuous upgrading of taste in America and in those nations that have
large industries to serve popular tastes. There is no excuse for sloppy
workmanship here, regardless of how lofty the purpose or how profound the insight. If it is worth saying, it is worth saying well,
technically. The aesthetic danger, however, is that of rejecting
Caruso recordings, because the fi is lo, or of exalting Herman Kaulbach's paintings, because the fi is hi. Hi-fi and academic painting
are therefore of a quality that places them in the same class of popular culture as best sellers, Broadway musicals and television "talk"
shows, all of which are slick in technique and sophisticated in content, two terms that are the merest hairsbreadth from weaning polished and profound. It is an important hairsbreadth aesthetically,
however; for the lines between slick and polished, between sophisticated and profound, are indicators of the difference between surface and texture. It is an important hairsbreadth intellectually,
too, for it is the difference between superficiality and depth. It is
an important hairsbreadth spiritually as well, for extrinsic price is
no more than a godless illusion of intrinsic worth.

Let us return to the visual arts industries that serve the popular public
made up of the two upward-striving strains, the newly enfranchised
and the status-panicked middle-class. In the 1890's, they were
served by expensive parlor editions of the academic arts of the World's
Fair. The academies themselves were industries that poured out stereotyped original works to serve the tastes of the new patrons, patrons
who wanted elevation, exclusiveness and clarity. Writing recently
of the period from 1890 to 1914, Therésé Burollet says "painting continued in the Third Republic as in previous centuries to tell a story
This role is no longer necessary: our need for images and evocation
is sated by photography, the cinema and television. Since Cecil B.
De Mille the historical reverie has been materialized at the level of
the masses and vast murals are no longer required." The problem,
though, is that while De Mille's art for the masses will satisfy the
popular needs for elevation and clarity, it won't satisfy the need for
exclusiveness. As C. Wright Mills said, if everybody belongs to the
fraternity, nobody gets any prestige from belonging. The new service
industry, for mass-produced prestige approached apogee in the early
1970's, and is seen at its most characteristic in the New Yorker magazine. The new popular exclusiveness, paradoxically, is that of the

limited edition.

The New Yorker, as everyone knows, was founded in 1925 on exclusive principles, symbolized by a stated original intention of not being for the little old lady in Dubuque. In unrelenting urbanity, mocking irony, tasteful conservatism, and polished obliqueness, the New Yorker has for half-a-century been a haven of social security for intellectuals and sophisticates. The popular pandering of its advertisements to the tastes of the nouveau-riche and sundry middle-brows are balanced with sophisticated anti-provincial fillers, anti-materialistic cartoons, and high prices in the advertisements.

Like the New Yorker, limited editions of art, too, have a long and honorable history. Etchings and woodcuts, for example, have always been limited in quality by the relatively short life of the block or the etching plate. Somewhat less limited are wood engraving and flatbed press printing; even less, steel engraving and lithography. In all of these mass-production art forms, there is artistry in the fact that the works are from an artist's hand, and there is exclusiveness in the fact that there is a natural limit to the output, caused by the diminution of quality after a certain degree of wear. This point may be reached as early as an edition of ten copies for drypoint etching or as late as several thousands for lithography and steel engraving. Additional artistry and exclusiveness can be added by hand coloring, artist's signatures, handmade watermarked paper, expensive bindings or frames, specially designed typefaces. All of these characteristics can be incorporated into aesthetic purpose and impact; but all can equally well be artificially imposed for arbitrary limitations. A particularly prevalent example of the latter is the mass production of original artworks by offset lithography, to be sold nationwide by mail-order clubs or through galleries. Offset lithography, of course, is virtually without limit in quality production potential. The exclusive value, therefore, is totally the result of artificial limitation, except where the edition includes the artist's autograph, and this rarely has any relevance to aesthetic value.

Similar to the limited edition service industry in prints and printing are commemorative ceramics, best known in Bing and Grondahl's Danish "Jul" plates. Names, dates, and numbers of plates are interesting, but not so important as the sentimental content of the

pictures. This can be illustrated easily with one of the many new
spin-off series -- take, for example, Svend Jensen of Denmarks's
Mors Dag -- with 1972 "Mother's Joy" @ $16.50; 1971 "Mother's
Love" @ $19.95; and 1970 "Bouquet for Mother" @ $22.50. These
1972 prices for the three Mother's Day plates will indicate the investment character of the plates. Even more blatantly materialistic
than series ceramics are the limited editions of precious-metal medal-
lions depicting great works of art and silver ingots stamped with presidential portraits and autographs, such as those that emanate from
sources like the Franklin Mint in Philadelphia. In these artifacts,
of course, feminine sentiment is eschewed, but they do bear in their
images the aura of certified arts. We may not be able to own Gil-
bert Stuart's portrait of George Washington, or an authentic signature
of Abraham Lincoln, but the exclusiveness of facsimiles in solid silver
is obviously a worthwhile alternative. More cultivated patrons of
arts will dismiss these limited editions as being no more than souvenir
collections (of which more later), but for the collectors they are a
key to becoming patron of the arts without the nervewracking strain
of making aesthetic judgments about intrinsic value. Furthermore,
the ingots do not detract from the patron's masculinity as collecting
Mother's Day plates would do. Their sentimental content is that of
the historical heritage, and history is always legitimately masculine.

The two characteristics of sentiment and investment are the primary
marks of the nouveau-riche limited edition New Yorker-sanctioned
popular art that promises exclusiveness to buyers. Some examples
will help to demonstrate their underlying aesthetics. Let's start at
the top. In 1973, in April, the New Yorker advertised a Steuben
Glass bowl -- no price quoted -- unmistakably art deco, and indeed,
first designed in 1935, engraved "by commission" forty-six times
since, by presumably nervous engravers, who were apparently clocked
for day of completion by the advertising executive, this one having
been completed on August 19, 1972. Individuality and quality are
beyond question, but the price is apparently unprintable. Two pages
later, four saccharine porcelain sculptures by Laszlo Ispanky. Prices,
printable -- $450, $500, $1500, $1500; but artistry unspeakable.
Every reprehensible characteristic of Third Republic academicians is
present: stereotyped idealistic faces, similar to Barbie and Ken dolls,
though somewhat weaker in character; crystal clear titles, with all
of the abstract nobility of the academy, viz., Spring Ballet, Spirit

of the Sea, Madame Butterfly and the Quest; technical quality, like
the films of De Mille, beyond criticism. The "editions," respectively,
are of 400, 450, 300 and 50.

This is beautiful art, we are to understand, both because the retail
sale value of goods on this page alone adds up to $930,000, and be-
cause the New Yorker prints the advertisement. Yet this was strange
modern art to purvey in 1973. Madame Butterfly is so Anglo-Saxon
in appearance that Lieutenant Pinkerton would hardly have been
discommoded in Dubuque by settling down with this Cio-Cio-San.
The Quest (@$1500) depicts a weirdly articulated male model in a
green diaper, with a rather "square" 1959 haircut, balanced goosily
upon a crescent moon, and in a position that must be abstract, for it
eludes anecdote. The medium in which his body exists is puzzling,
at least. If the medium is air, he is a dancer, but either the wind
blows the wrong way on his diaper, or, he will abrade his instep
upon landing. If his medium is water, his diaper still wafts wrongly.
If it is outer space, he is very poorly dressed. And whatever his
quest, he's found it, because he's got it in his hand.

These (almost) million-dollar art works in one of America's "most
sophisticated" magazines are the first example of kitsch in this book,
with the possible exception of the salt-and-pepper-shaker "Praying
Hands" of Dürer -- cost $1.98. Kitsch, as I have stated earlier,
always has a political dimension, but in the case of Laszlo Ispansky's
porcelains, it is a matter of politics by guilty association, for the
only clear design antecedents for The Quest are the "Aryan" art of
Nazi Germany and the slick proletarianism of Stalin's Soviet Union.

Enough of Ispanky. Ten pages later, the New Yorker advertises,
"Armstrong's Proudly Presents 'Goldilocks and the Three Panda Bears'
by Cybis." Prices: Goldilocks and one Panda Bear, $145.00; addi-
tional two Panda Bears, $75.00. These adorable porcelains are
right out of Walter Lantz' Andy Panda (Walt Disney being too severe),
and their exclusiveness is only in price and association with the New
Yorker.

Thirty pages later, we are back at Ispanky, this time for the Jewish
trade: "Aaron . . . brother of Moses. . . ." @ $1,200 in an
edition of 350, and replete in what is, vaguely, a Crusaders' garb,

163

an anachronism most improper for an academician. This is not the
end, however; the same magazine offers Antonia Borsat's Golden
Years, @ $1,450 per plate in a limited edition of 700 (that's a mil-
lion dollars, retail!): "FIRST 3-DIMENSIONAL commemorative
plate by world-famous sculptor of Milan, Italy. In ageless porcelain, individually hand colored with slight, but distinctive variance,
each plate is an original; each signed and numbered. Masterpiece
sic of this magnitude rarely available outside of museum collections." The picture is of the type of the Düsseldorf academy of 1870
or so, depicting an old man hobbling toward a coy old lady, all within an unkempt garden in 3 DIMENSIONS, making certain that "plate"
will be useless luxury.

In brief, therefore, the "academy" is far from dead. Whereas it began
as an institution to free the artist from the common herd by separating
him from mere craftsmanship and dedicating him to idealistic purpose,
the "academy" has shifted toward serving the popular tastes as those
tastes have become embodied in a well-to-do class of persons, eager
for cultivation. In style, these art works are like the old academic,
being realistic rather than expressionistic, anecdotal rather than abstract, ethereal rather than earthy. One might be tempted to label
the sentimentality of these arts as feminine, but this would only be
justifiable if we labeled the market aesthetic of contrived limited
editions as masculine. Similarly, one might like to label the whole
business as middle class, thus leaving inviolate both professional
sophisticates born to the purple on the one hand, and wholesomely
independent lowbrows on the other.

Labels simply won't work, though. If we expunge support from the
New Yorker and lower the prices, we will find the similarly contrived market of Avon collectables -- the almost current, yet obso-
lescent bottles and jars of the Avon Products' door-to-door cosmetics
trade (for which Avon publishes its own "antique" market quotations
for its salespeople); or Jim Beam whiskey decanters, which have a
delicacy equal to a 1943 Kewpie doll, and a market value close to
a Bing and Grondahl's 1963 Christmas plate. If, on the other hand,
we insist upon something deeper than regarding art as a medium for
status or investment, we cannot escape the leveling denominator of
collecting, the "anal instinct" of Freud's psychology, or what, in
popular culture terms, might be called the souvenir aesthetic.

Whether male or female, upper-class or lower, the anal instinct is shared by all in common.

Although my tone has been critical concerning these materialistic gatherings of investment art that are stereotyped imitations of fine arts and of aristocratic collectors, there must be something of value to them and to their owners. My personal feeling of revulsion toward Ispanky et al. is not so much caused by the inherent aesthetic short-comings of their products as it is by the support given to them by a materialistic establishment. The support and sanction of the establishment tries to make exclusive that which should be common to all. The fact that people of all degrees of training and sensitivity wish to possess material arts is the common denominator that brings us into one camp of humanity. We are like the woman in Kurt Vonnegut's Slaughterhouse Five, who, "like so many Americans, was trying to construct a life that made sense from things she found in gift shops."

One of the most deep-seated of human drives is the desire to bring home a souvenir, a token of remembrance of a past time and a distant space. More primitive creatures, such as pack-rats, magpies and children are instinctively drawn to shiny, colorful, out-of-the-ordinary objects that they snatch up to take to their nests, or their pockets, or their treasure chests. With increasing age, the souvenirs tend to lose the primitive haphazardness, and to become fixed in the socially-sanctioned form of manufactured souvenirs, such as sea-shell birds labeled "souvenir of Yellowstone National Park," or stenciled American flag throw-pillows, "Souvenir of Miami Beach;" or lac-quered cedar plaques with philosophic mottoes, designated as "Souvenirs of New York City." These are impersonal and stereotyped, yet their abundance is an indication of their ability to satisfy the need se souvenir, to "come up," that is, to summon up a memory.

The more sophisticated collectors of souvenirs try to personalize and to give order to their souvenir tokens. Matchbooks from local restaurants and businesses, picture post cards and luggage stickers are three of the oldest forms and serve as a conventional bridge between the official souvenir and more individualized collections such as some I recall from the past of several members of my family: local beer cans, newspaper mastheads and labels from bottles of wine consumed at out-of-town restaurants. A neighbor of ours used to buy a

pottery cow whenever she went to another town -- cows, it seems, are a popular motif, though not in the big leagues with cats, dogs, pigs and owls. All of these collections are true souvenirs, although all of them have the potential of growing into hobbies, in which the souvenir function is supplanted by more intellectualized study, with classification, comparison, analysis, discrimination and determination of aesthetic and market values providing a rational veneer to what remains a sublimated form of the primitive anal drive to accumulate. When this drive manifests itself in huge balls of string, we label it an aberration, when it is manifested in large bank accounts, we applaud it, when it appears in an art collection, we revere it.

The souvenir drive is different from mere accumulation of shiny objects. It seems to be rooted in a desire to arrest time and to dissolve space. It is, therefore, in a larger view, a quest for immortality, a denial of the continuum of time that unendingly relegates an infinity of <u>nows</u> into an eternity of <u>then</u>. The souvenir drive is an attempt to preserve happy presents in material symbols, in static metaphors of time. This is serious business, and regarded in this way, the purchase of a felt pennant -- "Souvenir of Niagara Falls" -- is an occasion that hints at the human tragedy. Man is mortal.

But all this may seem to be undue attention paid to vulgar objects, to cliché homilies, faddish banners, unfunny novelties and unlovely decorations. To these is due no honor, beyond the recognition of their functions as indicators of universal and dignified human needs to arrest time, to express individuality, to announce a sense of personal worth. Regrettably, and as I have stated before, far too often, the worth is presumed to be in the object, the individuality in the exclusiveness of the object, and the arresting of time in the monumental honor ascribed to the object. It is not so. The arresting of time in arts is only in the aesthetic moment of contemplation, inspiration, vision or joy. The object is not the message, but the medium. Some of these media will survive, because their messages are useful to humankind. Far more will be buried in the succession of old todays that we call history, only to regain a dubious dignity if decay all around renders them unique.

The value that results from accidental historical survival is unpredictable, of course. But the values produced by usefulness --

166

psychological, aesthetic and spiritual usefulness -- may help to point up the inherent dangers of the academic limited-edition aesthetics of the middle-brow nouveau-riche. They are investing in sure-fire losers that are big in size or in price, that are ostentatiously enhanced with applied detail, and that are, above all, incapable of evolution because they are lifeless.

Further, in their contrived exclusiveness, both patron and art are denied the lifegiving popular aesthetic with which this book began: that art which sells, is good popular art; that which doesn't sell, is not -- if there is a choice from among competing producers of popular arts. In such an open market there is continuous evolution. The history of this evolution is a litterheap of cast-off popular objects, each of which, in its day, had the life-giving capacity for expressing pleasurable meanings, along with extreme vulnerability in its evolutionary competition for lasting value. But lasting value of the popular art object is not guaranteed by protecting it from the competition by means of academies, restricted production, or useless specialization that separate it from the common denominators of humanity.

The few -- the very few -- survivors will survive because their specialization refreshes our comprehension of the common denominators. The special characteristics that demark each art object as being part of its time and place in the evolution of the arts are the numerators that surprise those common denominators that find expression in the best of all arts.

Throughout this book, I have taken delight in those boundless numerators of arts and history and social phenomena, but I hope that I have kept withal a touch of life and love of the eternal denominators of human beings, from the mouths and hands that make a Coke bottle right, to the sense of immediacy that gives life to television, to the bodies that strive for freedom in dance, to the icons of catalogs that express dreams of better life on earth, to the child's longing for reality and fantasy kept in balance, to the gardens in which we shape microcosms of our ideal worlds, to the human hand that makes all religious art one in whatever time or clime, to all the souvenir possessions that recall us into immortality for aesthetic instants in time. Discerning such common denominators in the junkpile of humanity is not an easy task, but it is well worth the doing, for what people

love is all there is of life, and what they dream, is all there is thereafter.

Afterword

An afterword is appropriate because the topics of this book have been
living cultural organisms that flex and grow, not dead issues that will
lie unchanging for the critic's scalpel.   These topics are living, yet
their manifestations are ephemeral, and so, much as I have attempted
to uncover human universals underlying the phenomena of the moment
and to put them into the company of historical antecedents and parallels, many of my illustrative examples will be dated.

This afterword, therefore, is an invitation to you to continue this
book by noting more recent evidence, both supporting and dissenting;
to continue it by refining, revising, correcting and extending the
topics and the interpretations; and to continue it by participating in
the popular arts as fully as you can, in whatever mode is most con-
genial to your life style. If you like to read criticism, read critics
and reviewers; if you like history, carry beyond my historical leads;
if you are a patron of the cultivated arts, enlarge your patronage to
include the outlaw arts. Do not abandon your objectivity, your
critical sense, your cultivation and your tastes: such abandonment

is uncalled for; but still give yourself generously and openly to the joys of the masses in plain and simple things, for, with Caliban (and I think with Will Shakespeare too), I say: "Be not afeard: the isle is full of noises, sounds, and sweet airs that give delight . . . and hurt not."

Bibliography

Chapter I

Throughout this book, I attempt to make most references self-explanatory. In some chapters, sources have been easy to document, but in others, research has been based upon "common knowledge" or upon direct experiences with anonymous or transient arts. The chapter bibliographies are not designed to be used as suggested reading lists nor as exhaustive last words on the topics. They represent sources actually used by allusion or by direct quotation. Naturally, many standard reference sources were consulted throughout.

Thompson, Denys, Discrimination and Popular Culture, Penguin, 1964.

Tebbel, John, "Britain's Troubled Air," Saturday Review, August 12, 1967.

Chapter 3

Some undocumented research derives from years of watching ballet and All Star Wrestling.

Bhavnani, Enakshi, The Dance in India, D. B. Taraporevala: Bombay, 1965.

Bosworth, Allan R., "Men to Match Japan's Mountains," Harpers, February, 1960.

Brean, Herbert, "Wrestling Script Gone Awry," Life, December 2, 1957.

Gallico, Paul, "That Was Acting," Theatre Arts, January, 1949.

Merleau-Ponty, Maurice, Sense and Non-Sense, Northwestern University Press: Evanston, 1964.

Nadel, Myron Howard and Constance Gwen Nadel, The Dance Experience; Readings in Dance Appreciation, Praeger: New York, 1970.

Palatsky, Eugene, "Meet Rick Starr: Wrestler With a Gimmick," Dance, May, 1963.

Sheets, Maxine, The Phenomenology of Dance, University of Wisconsin Press: Madison, 1966.

Walker, Benjamin, The Hindu World, Praeger: New York, 1968.

Chapter 4

Much of the research for this chapter was done in the various mail order catalogs that are referred to in the text. Several of these are recent facsimile reprints, many are in my own collection, others were consulted in the Home Economics library collection of the University of Minnesota in St. Paul.

Asher, Louis E. and Edith Heal, Send No Money, Argus: Chicago, 1942.

Emmet, Boris and John E. Jueck, Catalogs and Counters. A History of Sears, Roebuck and Company, University of Chicago Press: Chicago, 1950.

"Fitting Willie's Suit," Business Week, April 5, 1941.

Getlein, Frank, "Art at Sears," New Republic, April 20, 1903.

Grabar, Andre, Byzantine Painting, Skira: New York, 1953.

Milburn, George, "Catalogues and Culture," Good Housekeeping, April, 1946.

Miller, D. A., The Byzantine Tradition, Harper and Row: New York, 1966.

Paradise, Viola, "By Mail," Scribner's, April, 1921.

"Point of View," Scribner's, April, 1917.

Purinton, Edward Earle, "Satisfaction or Your Money Back," Independent, February 21, 1920.

"Sears Offers Art," Business Week, July 8, 1944.

Thompson, Lovell, "Eden in Easy Payments," Saturday Review of Literature, April 3, 1937.

Chapter 5

Primary research for this chapter was done at the Center for Research Libraries, the Scott, Foresman Company, the Whitman division of Western Publishing Company, the Hess Collection of the University of Minnesota, Minneapolis, and the curriculum collection of the University of Minnesota, Duluth. I have provided adequate bibliographical information on the primers in the text, and so omit them from this list.

Nietz, John A., "Why the Longevity of the McGuffey Readers?" History of Education Quarterly, June, 1964.

Smith, Nila Banton, American Reading Instruction, International Reading Association: Newark, Delaware, 1965.

Streitz, Ruth, and Dorothy Gradolf, "How Many Stories Are Repeated in the Primary Grades?" Childhood Education, May, 1930.

Tannenbaum, Abraham, "Family Living in Textbook Town," Progressive Education, March, 1954.

Chapter 6

Short titles are employed. A considerable amount of research was done in the catalogs of Sears, Roebuck and Company and of

Montgomery Ward, and in Sunset Magazine, Popular Mechanics, Popular Science, Better Homes and Gardens, Woman's Day and some other popular catalogs and periodicals. Other books were consulted for corroboration of popular trends, but it seems unnecessary to list them.

Beecher, Catherine E. and Harriet Beecher Stowe, The American Woman's Home, J. B. Ford: New York, 1869.

Cable, George Washington, The Amateur Garden, Scribner's: New York, 1914.

Cane, Percy S., Modern Gardens British and Foreign, Special Winter Number of "The Studio" 1926-27.

Clifford, Derek, A History of Garden Design (revised edition), Praeger: New York, 1966.

Downing, A. J., The Architecture of Country Houses, D. Appleton: New York, 1851.

Downing, A. J., A Treatise on the Theory and Practice of Landscape Gardening, Facsimile of 1859 Sixth Edition, Funk and Wagnalls: New York, 1967.

Dwyer, C. P., The Immigrant Builder Tenth Edition, Claxton, Remsem and Haffelfinger: Philadelphia, 1878.

Earle, Alice Morse, Old-Time Gardens, Macmillan: New York, 1967.

Eaton, Leonard K., Landscape Architect in America. The Life and Work of Jens Jensen, University of Chicago Press: Chicago, 1964.

Eaton, Walter Prichard, Everybody's Garden, Alfred A. Knopf: New York, 1932.

Edwards, Paul, English Garden Ornaments, G. Bell: London, 1965.

Farmer, Richard N., Farmer's Law. Junk in a World of Affluence, Stein and Day: New York, 1973.

Foley, Daniel J., The Complete Book of Garden Ornaments, Complements and Accessories, Crown: New York, 1972.

Garden Magazine, The, June, 1924. Special issue "Making the Garden Livable."

Gothein, Marie Luise, A History of Garden Art Vol. II, J. M. Dent: London, 1928.

Hadfield, Miles and John, Gardens of Delight, Cassell: London, 1964.

Hearth and Home, March 1, 1873; March 22, 1873.

Hedrick, U. P., A History of Horticulture in America to 1860, Oxford: New York, 1950.

Hibberd, Shirley, Rustic Adornments for Homes of Taste, Croombridge and Sons: London, 1856.

Hyams, Edward, A History of Gardens and Gardening, Praeger: New York, 1971.

King, Mrs. Francis, The Little Garden, Atlantic Monthly Press: Boston, 1921.

Loudon, Mrs. J. W., Gardening for Ladies, John Murray: London, 1843.

Lovell, Eleanor Cook, and Ruth Mason Hall, Index to Handicrafts, Modelmaking and Workshop Projects, F. W. Faxon: Boston, 1936, Supplements through 1967.

Manwaring, Elizabeth Wheeler, Italian Landscape in Eighteenth Century England, Oxford University Press: New York, 1925.

Olver, Edward W., Landscaping the Small Home, A. T. DeLaMare: New York, 1931.

Spring Hill Nurseries Catalog, Spring, 1974, Tipp City, Ohio.

175

Steele, Fletcher, Gardens and People, Houghton Mifflin: Boston, 1964.

Sutton, S. B., editor, Civilizing American Cities. A Selection of Frederick Law Olmstead's Writings on City Landscapes, MIT Press: Cambridge, 1971.

Tunnard, Christopher, and Henry Hope Reed, American Skyline, Mentor: New York, 1956.

Van Dommelen, David B. New Uses for Old Cannonballs, Funk and Wagnalls: New York, 1966.

Varney, Almon C., Our Homes and Their Adornments, J. C. Chilton: Detroit, 1883.

Walker Art Center, Naives and Visionaries, E. P. Dutton: New York, 1974.

Waugh, Frank A., Everybody's Garden, Orange Judd; New York, 1930.

Wheeler, Gervase, Homes for the People Revised edition, George E. Woodward: New York, 1867.

Wright, Mrs. Julia McNair, The Complete Home, (no publisher or place) 1889.

Wright, Richardson, The Story of Gardening (facsimile of 1934 edition), Dover: New York, 1964.

Chapter 7

Basic research for this chapter was done in religious book stores, Salvation Army stores, and St. Vincent de Paul stores.

Banerjea, Jitendra Nath, The Development of Hindu Iconography, University of Calcutta: Calcutta, 1956.

"Christian Stake in Dollar Power," <u>Christianity Today</u>, June 19, 1970.

Dillenberger, Jane, <u>Style</u> and <u>Content</u> in <u>Christian Art</u>, Abingdon: Nashville, 1965.

Ferguson, George, <u>Signs</u> and <u>Symbols</u> in <u>Christian Art</u>, Oxford: New York, 1966.

Giffords, Gloria Kay, <u>Mexican Folk Retablos: Masterpieces on Tin</u>, University of Arizona: Tucson, 1974.

Hind, Arthur M., <u>A History of Engraving and Etching</u> (1923), Dover: New York, 1963.

Jahn, Janheinz, <u>Muntu: The New African Culture</u>, Grove: New York, 1961.

Jones, Michael Owen, "The Useful and the Useless in Folk Art," <u>Journal of Popular Culture</u>, Spring, 1973.

Klein, Robert, and Henri Zerner, <u>Italian Art 1500-1600</u>, Prentice-Hall: Englewood Cliffs, 1966.

Maas, Jeremy, <u>Victorian Painters</u>, Putnams: New York, 1969.

Nochlin, Linda, <u>Realism and Tradition in Art 1848-1900</u>, Prentice-Hall: Englewood Cliffs, 1966.

"Peddlers of Paraphernalia," <u>Christian Century</u>, October 7, 1970.

Ray, Sudhausu Kumar, <u>The Folk-Art of India</u>, Yogalayan: Calcutta, 1967.

Chapter 8

References to magazine advertisements are largely included in the text.

Art and Artists of All Nations, Arkell Weekly Company: New York, 1894.

Dorfles, Gillo, et al., Kitsch. The World of Bad Taste, Universe Books: New York, 1969.

Gropius, Walter, The New Architecture and the Bauhaus, MIT Press: Cambridge, 1965.

Hess, Thomas B., and John Ashbery, Academic Art, Collier Books/ Art News: New York, 1971.

Pevsner, Nikolaus, Academies of Art Past and Present, Cambridge University Press: Cambridge, 1940.

Walton, William, World's Columbian Art and Architecture, George Barrie: Philadelphia, 1893.